Lessons Learned from World Bank Education Management Information System Operations

WORLD BANK STUDY

Lessons Learned from World Bank Education Management Information System Operations

System Operations

Portfolio Review, 1998–2014

Husein Abdul-Hamid, Namrata Saraogi, and Sarah Mintz

 WORLD BANK GROUP

Contents

Boxes

Figures

Map

Tables

Acknowledgments

This report was prepared by a team led by Husein Abdul-Hamid (Senior Education Specialist, World Bank Group) and composed of Namrata Saraogi and Sarah Mintz. The authors are grateful to World Bank peer reviewers, who were immensely helpful in guiding the content and direction of the paper: Peter Darvas (Senior Economist), Lianqin Wang (Senior Education Specialist), Laurence Wolff (International Education Consultant), and Hongyu Yang (Senior Education Specialist).

The team is especially thankful to World Bank colleagues Cristian Aedo (Practice Manager, Education Global Practice), Dandan Chen (Program Leader, Education Global Practice), Dingyong Hou (Senior Education Specialist, Education Global Practice), and Anh Lan Vu (Education Specialist, Education Global Practice), who participated in interviews and shared their time and technical expertise with the team. The team would also like to thank those who provided valuable inputs to this document: Jung-Hwan Choi, Jennifer Klein, Michael John Melamed, Cassia C. Miranda, and Wouter Takkenberg.

Executive Summary

This report provides an overview of the World Bank's portfolio in the area of Education Management Information Systems (EMISs) over 17 years from 1998 to 2014. It seeks to identify overall trends and characteristics of World Bank support in this area, with the intent of informing future project preparation and analytical work. Although several good practices were evident, operational performance of EMIS activities fell short of expectations, with widespread deficiencies that ranged from unclear definitions and understanding of EMIS to ineffective implementation and utilization. Future projects could benefit from the SABER-EMIS Paper.[1] The SABER-EMIS framework focuses on the need for (a) a strong enabling environment, (b) system soundness, (c) quality data, and (d) effective utilization as the key factors essential for the successful implementation of EMIS. This initial needs assessment of a country's EMIS can play a critical role in benchmarking countries and provide a valuable foundation for the design of new projects.

Examples of successful EMIS activities include (a) development of an EMIS to manage teachers and provide access to education (for example, Afghanistan); (b) utilization of an EMIS as a management tool (for example, Bosnia and Herzegovina); (c) creation of an online EMIS to improve access to education data (for example, Honduras); (d) use of an EMIS as a tool to strengthen teaching and learning (for example, Guatemala and Lithuania); and (e) use of an EMIS as a management tool for schools (for example, Malaysia). These success stories highlight how a well-implemented EMIS can improve the performance of an education system.

At the same time, numerous challenges have been identified as factors contributing to the shortcomings of EMIS-related projects. These include the following:

1. **Misalignment of Activities and Unrealistic EMIS Goals:** The portfolio review of projects reveals a frequent mismatch between the realities of a country's EMIS, including the country's capacity to implement EMIS, and the intended goals/indicators of the EMIS component set to be achieved by the project.
   - In some cases, governments did not have a clear understanding of the function of an EMIS throughout the implementation of the projects. Harmonization of EMIS goals, the overall project objectives, and government initiatives (for example, Albania) was lacking.

- In other cases, the EMIS activity was tied to the monitoring and evaluation (M&E) component of the project. Including an EMIS as part of M&E makes it less sustainable in the future because investment in the EMIS is made only to monitor the implementation status of that project. Once the project is completed, resources invested in the system are withdrawn, making it obsolete (for example, Pakistan).
- The amount of money allocated to the EMIS component was not explicitly stated in the project documents and, in some cases, not proportional to the tasks set to be implemented. The average EMIS share ranged from less than 1–10 percent of the total cost, which is often too low to design a new EMIS in a country (see figure 1.8).

2. **Institutionalization of the EMIS:** Projects did not focus on developing standards/mechanisms to institutionalize and operationalize the EMIS.
   - None of the reviewed projects focused on developing EMIS-specific policies. A strong legal framework is needed to guide the implementation work and ensure continuity of operations and long-term sustainability.
   - The focus of projects was more on the procurement of technology for EMIS development (such as purchasing software, hardware, and equipment) and less on the people and processes surrounding the technology (for example, Lebanon). Systems do not need to be over-designed or complicated. Building a sound information system requires a strong legal framework, clear working processes, reliable data, and effective data utilization. Thus, it is important to take a systemic approach to EMIS development, balancing the technical as well as the political, organizational, and human resource management issues.
   - Lack of investment was found in the training and professional development activities of the staff using the system. EMIS units within governments need continuous training on how to use the EMIS effectively and efficiently. Moreover, trainings and regular discussions should be held with school staff to inculcate a culture of data-driven decision making.
   - Poor data quality was a common problem due to lack of measures adopted to verify the accuracy of data provided by schools. In many cases, discrepancies were found in data at the regional and central government levels (for example, Chad). Appointing government officers at each level of the education system (schools, local, regional, and central) and developing automated validation mechanisms for quality assurance purposes would go a long way in improving data quality.
   - In most countries, separate offices and information systems are used for the EMIS, M&E, human resources (teacher roster), infrastructure, and assessments. Therefore, a stronger focus should be given to these parallel systems of EMIS, M&E, and other data generated and collected for real decisions. Also, often the coding among these systems (school IDs, student IDs, teacher IDs) is not harmonized, and so data cannot be consolidated. As a result, a considerable amount of time goes into consolidation of basic education data

on schools, teachers, and students collected by the Ministry of Education, Ministry of Finance, and Statistical Services.

- EMIS systems may overwhelm the Ministry staff and distract their attention from other, equally important management activities. In some countries, for example, for about six months, half of the Ministry is only collecting, analyzing, and presenting information (for example, Ghana). A better model might be to computerize data collection and subcontract analysis to local academic or research groups.

- In most countries, the initial EMIS cost is borne by international donor organizations. It is important that this initial investment is accompanied by sustained government investment to continue and maintain EMIS activities. In many countries, EMIS activity comes to a standstill after the project is completed, making continuity of EMIS operations impossible. The government should have a separate budget dedicated to EMIS activities, and the donor funding should be channeled through the government systems to provide transparency. Moreover, World Bank support should be withdrawn in a phased manner through an exit strategy that is closely tied to ongoing capacity building for the government.

3. **Sustainability Challenges Resulting from Inconsistent Leadership:** Many projects experienced changes in leadership, which, in turn, resulted in continuous revisions to the EMIS objectives. Multiple revisions to goals weaken government support and create problems in implementation (for example, Bolivia). As a consequence, the EMIS component carries forward to the next project, without any subsequent successes.

4. **Missed Integration Opportunities:** Some projects invested in setting up different information systems without considering the need to integrate them (for example, Eritrea). In other cases, different modules were developed under the same EMIS system without linking them. Understanding these systems as one comprehensive EMIS can help reduce costs, improve data utilization, and eliminate inefficient spending that channels scarce resources to the operations of multiple systems.

5. **Private Players in Education:** Another key problem faced by projects is capturing information from the private sector. In countries such as Ghana and Nigeria, the private sector is dominant and the consequences of being rendered visible by EMIS are questionable; the reluctance of the private sector to participate fully makes the EMIS unreliable. Governments should find ways to incentivize private schools to supply accurate data for reporting.

6. **EMIS at Local Levels:** Projects mainly focused on developing an EMIS at the central level as a tool for planning by the Education Ministry. An EMIS should not be just about the central government and development partners such as the World Bank and USAID; it is also about local governments, schools, and communities. It should be seen as a tool for improving learning and instruction, and increasing the information flow back to subnational, institutional, and client levels for building local oversight and social accountability.

Based on these operational challenges, numerous lessons have been offered to constructively inform and guide World Bank task teams on the effective design and implementation of an EMIS at each stage of the project cycle.

Project Preparation

1. Conducting a needs assessment of the EMIS before the start of the project would be beneficial to understand the current need for an EMIS to inform and guide project preparation. Implementation of an EMIS in low-income, low-capacity countries is different from in middle-income, higher-capacity countries, perhaps with computerized systems. The scale and scope need to be adjusted to the local capacities and economic and financial conditions. SABER-EMIS can be a valuable tool in making some of the key decisions. These include determining the availability and capacity of staff directly responsible for the EMIS, examining the resources going into it, and ascertaining the extent of high-level buy-in, as well as technical issues such as the current software platform(s) being used, database management, and the compatibility of the system with other education databases in the Ministry for integration purposes that could be instrumental in the project design.
2. The project teams should have a clear understanding of the EMIS goals, and these goals should align with the project costs, overall project objective, and government needs.
3. Project teams should follow a systematic procedure in executing EMIS activities. As a first step, EMIS policies should be identified, and any gaps should be addressed. Second, stakeholders' needs and aspirations should be identified to design a system that would be effectively utilized by them, for example, a user-friendly interface for parents, students, and teachers to access data. Third, systematic procedures should be adopted for the procurement of software, hardware, and other tools. Fourth, it is important to think of the identifiers needed for integration of databases. Fifth, security and validation mechanisms should be enforced to protect against data thefts. Finally, data should be open and accessible to the public.
4. A strong commitment from the government is needed to implement the system and ensure its long-term sustainability.
5. Steps should be taken to ensure that the EMIS's full potential is realized. An EMIS should be seen as a tool for teaching and learning, as well as for compliance.

Operational Phase

1. The time lag between the launch of the project and its implementation should be reduced to ensure a strong start. Task team leaders should avoid continuous changes in EMIS goals during implementation.
2. Capacity-building exercises should take place throughout the operational phase and should be designed and budgeted so that they can continue on a

regular and ongoing basis. Professional development activities should encompass necessary technical training for relevant staff at all levels of the education system (including top-level decision makers, local-level teachers, principals, and journalists), as well as training on EMIS policies, processes, and utilization. Steps should be taken to ensure that the data collected and stored in the EMIS are made available to the relevant stakeholders in the country.

3. Government officers should be appointed to verify the quality of data collected from schools. Doing this would reduce delays in data collection at the school level, as well as improve the quality of data collected.

4. Dissemination strategies should be strengthened to make data available to the relevant stakeholders through newspapers, magazines, the Internet, and books, in the process making the government accountable for the published data.

5. Regular discussions and training sessions should be held in schools with principals and teachers to create a culture of data-driven decision making in their core operations. Ongoing communication is needed with all levels of the education system on the vision for the EMIS, as well as ongoing implementation updates. Building a data-driven culture in many countries can take up to 20 years, so continuous efforts should be made by the government to create and foster that culture.

Project Completion

1. World Bank and donor support should be reduced in a phased manner, with continuing support to provide help to improve local capacity.

2. Research and development activities and incentives should be encouraged to promote the utilization of the system.

Note

1. SABER-EMIS Framework Paper: http://wbgfiles.worldbank.org/documents/hdn/ed /saber/supporting_doc/Background/EMIS/Framework_SABER-EMIS.pdf.

Abbreviations

BEIS	Basic Education Information System
CTS	Child Tracking Survey
DISE	District Information System for Education
EMIS	Education Management Information System
EPU	Education Planning Unit
EQUIP	Education Quality Improvement Program
ESSP	Education Sector Support Project
HEMIS	Higher Education Management Information Systems
HMIS	Health Management Information System
ICR	Implementation Completion Report
IMU	Information Management Unit
ISR	Implementation Status Report
KPIs	key performance indicators
M&E	monitoring and evaluation
MEC	Ministry of Education and Culture
MEHE	Ministry of Education and Higher Education
MES	Ministry of Education and Science
MIS	Management Information System
MoE	Ministry of Education
MRIS	Material Resources Information System
PAD	project appraisal document
PID	project information document
SABER	Systems Approach for Better Education Results
SEP	Secretariat of Public Education
SEPE	State-Level Secretariats of Public Education
SIS	Student Information System
TA	technical assistance
UBE	universal basic education

Background: What Is an EMIS?

An Education Management Information System (EMIS), in its simplest form, can be defined as a system responsible for collection, maintenance, analysis, dissemination, and utilization of data in an education system. EMISs vary dramatically across countries. In fact, each country is different, and within a country often additional variation is seen at the local school system level. Among the most significant factors driving variation are the political framework in which the EMIS functions, technological means, and differences in the culture around data and types of data utilization. This document identifies three core stages of EMIS development: (1) accountability and compliance, (2) instruction and management, and (3) intelligent and integrated. In practice, countries may be between stages, exhibiting characteristics of multiple stages at one time; however, key differences exist in the type of data collected and how the data are managed and utilized that constitute each stage. Stage 1 of EMIS development, accountability and compliance, refers to a simple flow of student information from schools to the central government, with limited production of reports such as school profiles or student enrollment information. Stage 2, learning and management, includes accountability and compliance capabilities as well as greater sophistication in collection and management of instructional data such as formative/summative assessments, special needs data, or projections of students at risk of dropping out and management information such as school finances and staff evaluations. Stage 2 also introduces feedback loops through which governments share information back to local school systems and communities. Stage 3, intelligent and integrated, includes capabilities from stages 1 and 2, as well as analytics and business intelligence services and integration of a K-12 EMIS with information systems in other government agencies such as higher education and labor agencies. Additionally, reporting and analysis provide quality data on a timely schedule to all levels of the education system.

Stage 1: Accountability and Compliance

Stage 1 of EMIS development is simple. It comprises student information chan-
neling from local schools to the central government (figure B.1). Student information includes demographic data such as gender and age, as well as data on
enrollment and drop-out rates, ideally by grade at each school. Stage 1 does not
require advanced technology. In some cases, data are collected in paper form and
carried to the school system or central government office, where the data are
manually added to the EMIS database. In most cases, this stage does not include
high levels of utilization, especially at the local level. One reason for this is that
policies and processes that make feedback loops for information to flow back to
the local level are rarely found. Even without feedback loops and advanced technology, opportunities exist for principals and teachers to use school data for more
than just reporting student information to the government. Projects that develop
these utilization skills will help build a strong foundation upon which the EMIS
can quickly and effectively advance. The more that principals and teachers use
data, even data recorded on paper, the more prepared they will be when technological resources are deployed.

Basic EMIS implementation can be easier to implement and utilize, because
users are not struggling with issues of system integration and other technological
constraints and because users are generally working with smaller datasets. This
stage of EMIS development should have a long-term vision and strategy. Special
attention should be given to the following:

- Alignment with the trajectory of EMIS development into subsequent stages,
  including an EMIS implementation timeline
- Training for stakeholders (teachers, headmasters, parents, policy makers, and
  others) on the value of data and how to use it and
- Design of a simple set of indicators that can grow over time.

Figure B.1 Stage 1: Accountability and Compliance

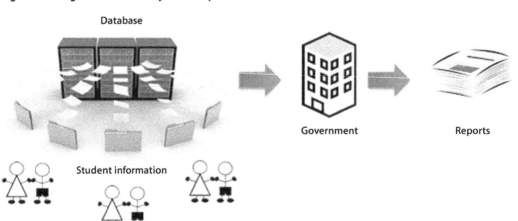

Lessons Learned from World Bank Education Management Information System Operations
http://dx.doi.org/10.1596/978-1-4648-1056-5

Stage 2: Instruction and Management

Stage 2 of EMIS development introduces the collection, management, and utilization of instructional learning data (figure B.2). This is an important advancement in system functionality because it transitions the EMIS from a focus of reporting data, usually for compliance purposes, to the government, and it moves into utilization of an EMIS to improve learning outcomes for students. Part of this transition also includes using the EMIS to make the work of teachers, principals, and administrators more efficient, through smarter allocation of money, resources, and time.

Instructional data include grades and assessment scores (both formative and summative assessments), as well as data on specific learning needs such as special needs, language issues, and even data relating to socioeconomic status of the student's family. This level of insight transforms the work of teachers significantly because they are able to know how well students are absorbing lessons. Data reveal if a single student or a subgroup of students are struggling with material, or if the teacher is not effectively communicating the lesson. Teachers can also know whether a student is not grasping the information because of absences or as a result of unique learning needs. Likewise, instructional data transform the work of principals and administrators, who are better prepared to manage their staff, design professional development programs, or allocate resources. The addition of instructional data into an EMIS marks a fundamental shift in the delivery of instruction.

Another important element in stage 2 of EMIS development is the introduction of feedback loops, through which the government shares information with

Figure B.2 Stage 2: Instruction and Management

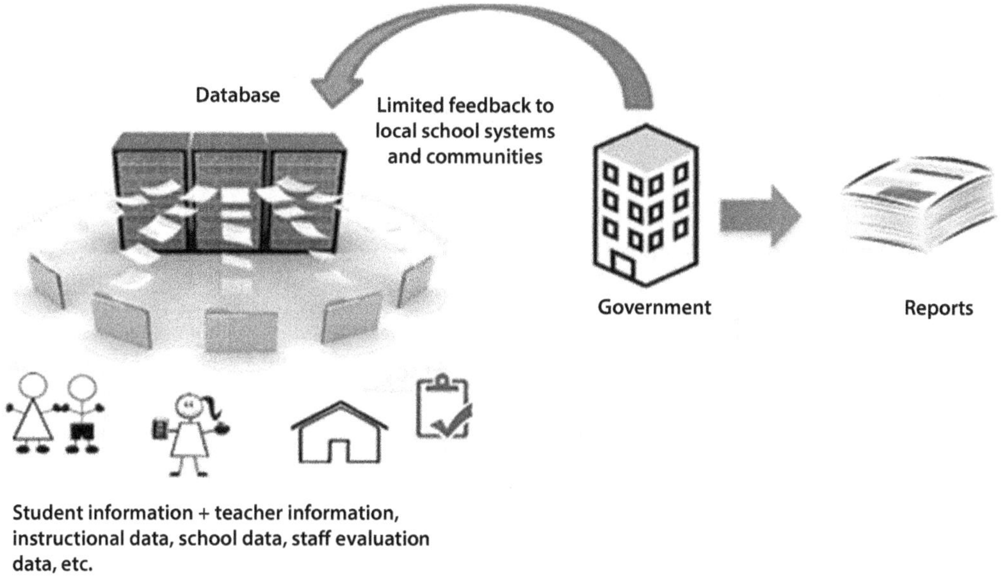

Database

Limited feedback to
local school systems
and communities

Government

Reports

Student information + teacher information,
instructional data, school data, staff evaluation
data, etc.

Lessons Learned from World Bank Education Management Information System Operations
http://dx.doi.org/10.1596/978-1-4648-1056-5

school systems. This may take the form of school profiles, enrollment information and trends, or even news articles that share learning outcomes of local school systems. Research shows that such transparency in information can improve accountability as well as student learning outcomes. Feedback loops during stage 2 are limited and do not yet contain more actionable and sophisticated information-sharing mechanisms such as real-time dashboards, mobile applications, or advanced statistical analysis (e.g., gradebooks or annual reports).

Stage 2 establishes the EMIS in the area of learning, increasing the capacity of the system to understand, analyze, and impact student learning outcomes. For education stakeholders who are implementing an EMIS in stage 2 of development, key topics to keep in mind include the following:

- Training in how to understand and utilize data remains critically important. Additionally, if feedback loops provide information to communities, projects should also train communities how to interpret public data.
- At this point technological systems are steadily advancing, meaning that attention should be paid to system soundness (processes and structures of the EMIS are sound and support the components of an integrated system) and data quality (processes for collecting, saving, producing, and utilizing information ensures accuracy, security, and high-quality, timely, and reliable information for use in decision making).

Stage 3: Intelligent and Integrated

Stage 3 of EMIS development includes all aspects of stage 2 and introduces data and utilization for management of the education system at all levels (figure B.3). Management includes data on administration, human resources, and finances, as well as business intelligence and analytics that empower education stakeholders with the applications, infrastructure, tools, and best practices that enable access to and analysis of information to improve and optimize decisions and performance. An important aspect of stage 3 is that the EMIS is fully established across all four policy areas (enabling environment, system soundness, quality data, and utilization for decision making). With the EMIS fully established, it is now able to extend its utility by integrating with systems outside of the K-12 education system. This could include implementation of a longitudinal data system, which integrates with higher education management information systems (HEMISs) and workforce data to track the progression of students through the education system and into the workforce.

This type of integration provides insight into the education system and allows policy makers to answer questions such as the following:

- Are students academically prepared to enter postsecondary institutions and complete their programs in a timely manner?
- Which government programs are most effective in improving access and success (i.e., retention and graduation) for students?

Figure B.3 Stage 3: Intelligent and Integrated

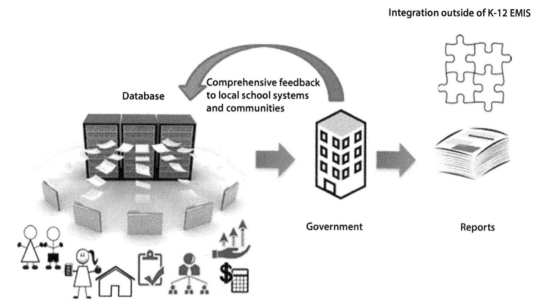

- Are community college students able to transfer within the state to four-year institutions successfully and without loss of credit?
- Which four-year institutions are graduating students most effectively and in the timeliest fashion?
- Are postsecondary and tertiary graduates successful in the workforce?
- What are the workforce outcomes of students who drop out of school?

Stage 3 of EMIS development supports the highest levels of efficiency and effectiveness across the education system, with regard to both instructional practices as well as management practices. At this level, the EMIS is full institutionalized into the education system, and utilization spans a wide variety of areas within and beyond the K-12 education system.

Stage 3 establishes EMIS in the area of learning and management, establishing the system as a central tool in both instruction and management. For education stakeholders who are implementing EMIS in stage 3 of development, key topics to keep in mind include the following:

- Agreements with external stakeholders
- Continuing to innovate and expand feedback loops to local systems (apps, more data, more training)
- Training and utilization of analytics and business intelligence.

Lessons Learned from World Bank Education Management Information System Operations
http://dx.doi.org/10.1596/978-1-4648-1056-5

CHAPTER 1

Overview of World Bank EMIS Activities

Introduction and Methodology

Assessing the state of education in a country demands information about the inputs, resources, governance, operations, and outcomes of its education system. An education management information system (EMIS) provides systematic, quality data in a well-structured enabling environment that facilitates utilization of the information produced in planning and policy dialogue (Abdul-Hamid 2014). The World Bank Education Portfolio includes more than 415 activities in developing countries since 1998. Out of these, 236 (57 percent) have an EMIS activity, reflecting strong recognition of the importance of EMIS (map 1.1).[1] This report reviews all 236 World Bank Education activities, analyzing the challenges and lessons learned, as conveyed in the project documents.

The report also reviews the Bank's support for EMISs through the lens of the EMIS Framework Paper "What Matters for Education Management Information Systems," recently developed by the Bank under the Systems Approach for Better Education Results (SABER) initiative (Abdul-Hamid 2014).

SABER helps countries assess their education systems and benchmark them against those of other countries through its worldwide data on policies and institutions. SABER-EMIS assesses education information systems with the aim of informing dialogue on policies related to education statistics and indicators, as well as to help countries monitor overall progress related to educational inputs, processes, and outcomes (Abdul-Hamid 2014). SABER-EMIS has identified four policy goals that are essential to EMIS design:

- **Enabling environment:** The policies, structure, human resources, and culture surrounding an EMIS that ensure collection, processing, and dissemination of data.
- **System soundness:** The architecture, processes, and integration capabilities of an EMIS, along with the comprehensiveness of the data collected by the system.

Map 1.1 World Bank EMIS Operations (1998–2014)

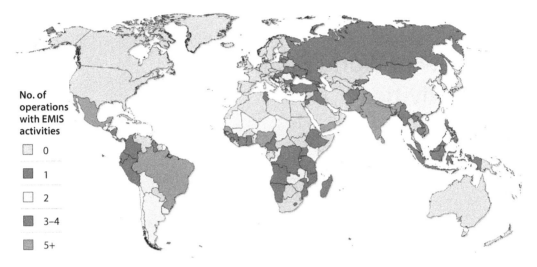

No. of
operations
with EMIS
activities

☐ 0
■ 1
☐ 2
■ 3–4
▨ 5+

Source: World Bank Education Projects Database.

- **Quality data:** The procedures that ensure the collection of reliable, accurate, and timely data for decision-making purposes.
- **Utilization for decision making:** The extent to which the data produced by an EMIS is used by different stakeholders (principals, teachers, parents, students, and governments) across the education system.

Using the World Bank Education Statistics website (EdStats),[2] information and analysis in this report draw from an extensive review of project documents including Project Appraisal Documents (PADs), Project Information Documents (PIDs), and Implementation Status Reports (ISRs). In addition, Implementation Completion Reports (ICRs) of closed operations were analyzed to inform the implementation status and progress of relevant projects.

Overview of the World Bank Education Portfolio

Since 2000, World Bank lending for education has averaged approximately US$2.2 billion annually, accounting for 8 percent of the total World Bank IBRD and IDA commitment (figure 1.1). The largest number of education projects have been undertaken in the Africa region, followed by South Asia and the Middle East and North Africa (World Bank 2014 Education Statistics Database).

As of June 2015, 144 projects are active in the education global practice, amounting to $14.2 billion in the portfolio. Table 1.1 shows the World Bank's education portfolio from 2007 to 2013.

Figure 1.1 Education Commitments by IBRD and IDA, FY 2000–15

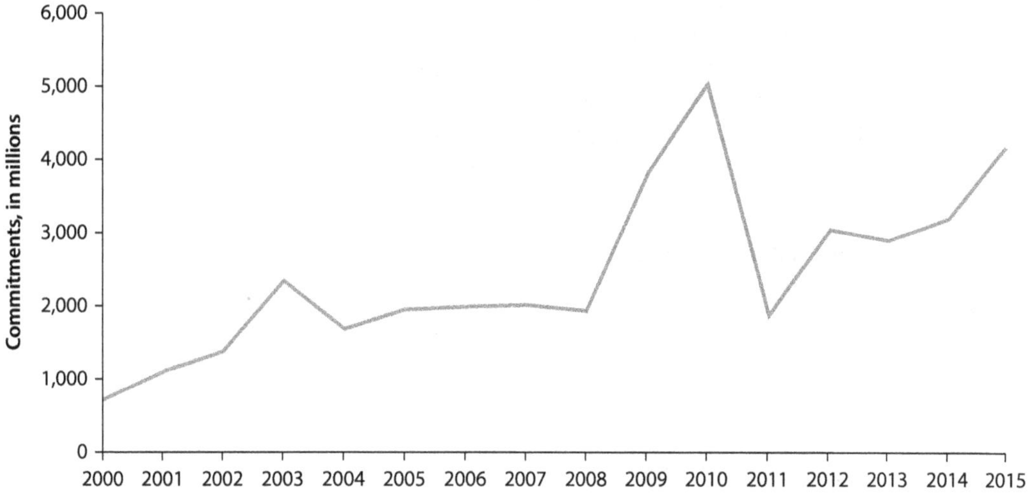

Source: World Bank 2014 Education Statistics Database.

Table 1.1 Education Portfolio (FY 2007–13)

	FY07	FY08	FY09	FY10	FY11	FY12	FY13
Number of active education projects	131	141	152	142	142	132	126
Number of countries	88	90	86	81	79	73	72
IBRD commitments (US$ million)	3,843	3,232	3,552	4,509	3,624	2,703	2,235
IDA commitments (US$ million)	3,579	4,130	5,151	6,448	6,682	5,598	6,289
Recipient-executed trust fund* (US$ million)		310	754	705	825	780	771
Special financing (US$ million)	10	10	10	20	20	27	12
Net commitments (US$ million)	7,432	7,681	9,467	11,682	11,151	9,107	9,306
Education projects as % of total bank portfolio	9%	9%	9%	8%	8%	8%	8%
Education commitments as % of total bank commitments	7%	7%	7%	7%	7%	5%	5%

Source: World Bank 2014 Education Statistics Database: http://datatopics.worldbank.org/education/.
Note: IBRD = International Bank for Reconstruction and Development; IDA = International Development Association.

Education Portfolio through the Lens of EMIS

Since 1998, the World Bank has extended support to 236 projects with an EMIS component. Of these 236 projects, 150 are closed and 86 are currently active (figure 1.2).

The two regions with the highest number of EMIS projects are Sub-Saharan Africa (SSA) and Latin America and the Caribbean (LAC). Brazil and Bangladesh undertook the most EMIS activities (13 projects each). Figure 1.3 illustrates the breakdown of projects, by region.

For 133 closed projects for which ICR ratings were available, 70 (52 percent) were rated satisfactory or higher, 42 (32 percent) were moderately satisfactory, and only 21 projects (16 percent) were unsatisfactory. For 71 active projects for which ISR ratings were available, 35 (49 percent) projects were rated satisfactory,

Figure 1.2 World Bank EMIS Activities, 1998–2013

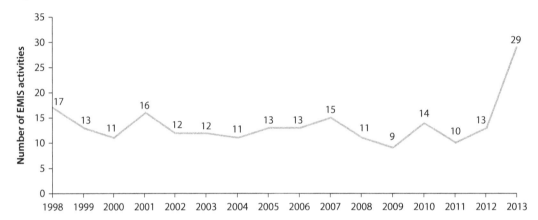

Figure 1.3 World Bank EMIS Activities, by Region

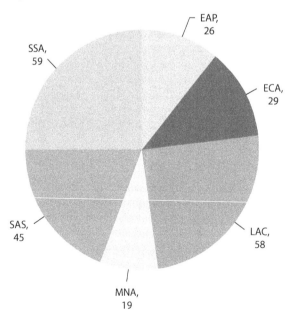

Note: EAP = East Asia and Pacific, ECA = Europe and Central Asia, LAC = Latin America and Caribbean, MNA = Middle East and North Africa, SAS = South Asia, SSA = Sub-Saharan Africa.

27 (38 percent) were moderately satisfactory, and only 9 projects (13 percent) were unsatisfactory (figure 1.4).

For 62 closed projects for which EMIS ratings were available, 30 projects (48 percent) were rated satisfactory, 14 projects (22 percent) were moderately satisfactory, and 18 projects (30 percent) were unsatisfactory (figure 1.5).

The average cycle of a project ranges from four to seven years (figure 1.6). Out of the 220 projects for which information on approval and closing dates were available, 158 projects (66 percent) had an average cycle of four to seven years, 17 projects lasted for eight years or more, and three projects closed during the same year of their approval (figure 1.4). It is interesting to note that longer-term

Figure 1.4 Project Ratings, Active and Closed Projects

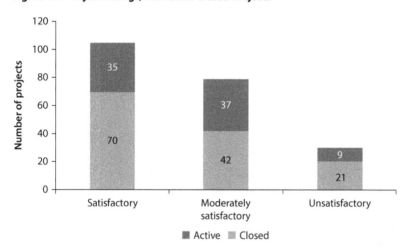

Figure 1.5 EMIS Ratings, Closed Projects

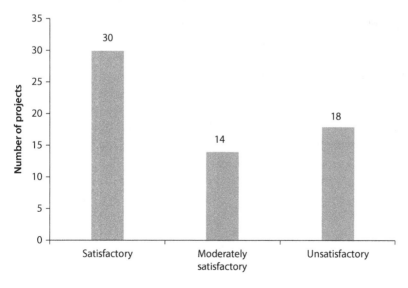

Lessons Learned from World Bank Education Management Information System Operations
http://dx.doi.org/10.1596/978-1-4648-1056-5

Figure 1.6 Average Cycle of Projects

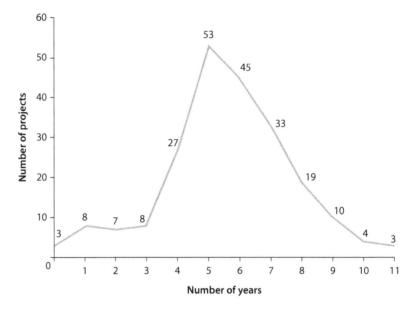

projects do not necessarily have better results in development of an EMIS. Projects that lasted for 10–11 years did not develop a well-functioning EMIS. Major technical, operational, and data quality issues were associated with the information system.

This report categorizes EMIS activities undertaken within each project into four groups based on the description available in the project documents: (1) strengthening an EMIS, (2) developing an EMIS, (3) upgrading an EMIS, and (4) assessing an EMIS (figure 1.7). Results show that 91 projects were dedicated to strengthening an EMIS, 82 projects focused on developing an EMIS, seven projects focused on upgrading an EMIS, and only three projects focused on assessing an EMIS.

1. **Strengthening an EMIS** includes activities to improve the capacity of the existing system by, for example, increasing personnel, improving infrastructure, expanding the number of education statistics collected, and providing training to staff. This group was further classified into three categories:
   - *General classification* includes a broad range of activities (mentioned above) undertaken to strengthen the existing system
   - *Integration* includes activities that focused on linking or integrating the existing information system with other information systems to make it more comprehensive
   - *Monitoring and evaluation* (M&E) includes an EMIS as a subcomponent of the M&E component where the EMIS was strengthened to improve the M&E mechanisms for tracking the overall progress of the project.

Figure 1.7 Breakdown of EMIS Activities

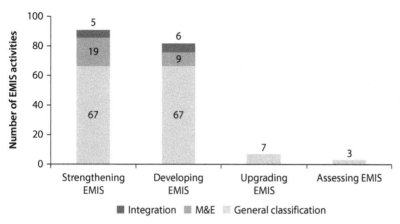

Note: EMIS = Education Management Information System; M&E = monitoring and evaluation.

On average, the amount of money spent on strengthening an EMIS ranged from less than $1 million to $5 million per project.

2. **Developing an EMIS** includes activities to establish an EMIS such as purchasing equipment, software, hardware, and other essential resources. This activity was further categorized into three groups:
   - *General classification* includes a broad range of activities undertaken to develop an EMIS, such as the collection of baseline data, establishing procedures, conversations with stakeholders, and purchase of equipment and other essential resources
   - *Integration* includes activities such as interoperability of systems
   - *M&E* includes activities where developing/establishing an EMIS was a subcomponent of the M&E component and where the EMIS was built to monitor the implementation status of the project.

On average, the amount spent on developing an EMIS ranged from less than $1 million to $7 million, per project.

3. **Upgrading an EMIS** includes activities that modernize the existing system such as change in the design, structure, and technology to a more advanced level. On average, the amount of money spent on upgrading an EMIS was less than $5 million per project.
4. **Assessing an EMIS** includes conducting studies and assessments to understand the current design and needs of the information system. On average, the amount of money spent on assessing an EMIS was less than $1 million per project.

The amount of money spent on the EMIS component varies from 0.5 to 21 percent of the total project cost (figure 1.8). Countries such as Latvia, Mali,

Figure 1.8 EMIS Share, as a Percentage of Project Cost

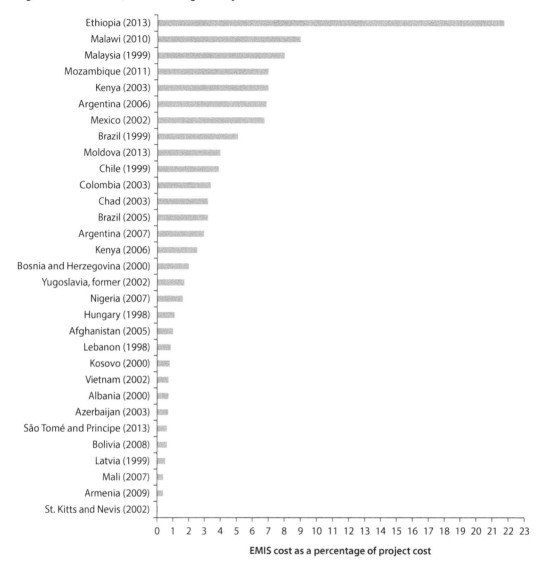

EMIS cost as a percentage of project cost

and St. Kitts and Nevis that spent less than 1 percent of the total project cost on an EMIS have not been successful in establishing an EMIS. Interestingly, even countries such as Ethiopia, which spent around 21 percent of their budget on EMIS, did not succeed in its successful implementation.

Mapping the number of EMIS activities to the basic reporting of education data, a few interesting patterns emerge (figure 1.9):

• Countries such as Mexico, Nepal, Pakistan, and Sri Lanka that had more than five EMIS activities during 1998–2014 reported a 100 percent data capture

Figure 1.9 Reporting of Basic Education Indicators (2009–13)

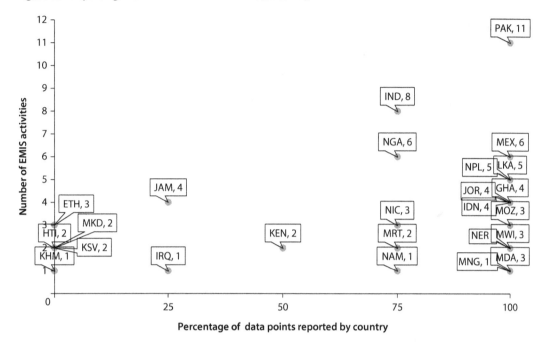

Source: World Bank 2014 Education Statistics Database.
Note: Basic Education Indicators include (a) Primary Completion Rate; (b) Net Enrollment Rate (Primary); (c) Gender Parity Index for gross enrolment (Primary); and (d) Youth (15–24) Literacy Rate, which are used for reporting Millennium Development Goals (MDGs).

of basic education indicators, showing signs of success in implementation of EMIS activities.

- On the other hand, countries in which Bank involvement was very low (fewer than three activities over the last 17 years) reported almost no data on education statistics. These countries include Cambodia, Ethiopia, Haiti, and Kosovo.
- On the other hand, countries such as India and Nigeria reported only 75 percent of the data on basic education, reflecting how EMIS activities need attention.

Based on the ICR reports, the status of implementation of EMIS activities were categorized into successes and challenges for 103 closed projects.[3] The challenges were further classified into four groups based on the nature of the problem: (1) management issues, (2) data quality issues, (3) technological issues, and (4) operational issues (figure 1.10). These four challenges and success stories are explained in more detail in the following section.

Each of the implementation issues was further classified into different categories to explain the root cause of the problem (figure 1.11). Data reveal that maximum challenges were faced during operations for various reasons, such as lack of adequate funding, limited training opportunities, and coordination issues across different units of the government. Other challenges related to weak capacity issues, poor quality of data, and untimely production and dissemination of data as well as limited utilization of the data produced.

Lessons Learned from World Bank Education Management Information System Operations
http://dx.doi.org/10.1596/978-1-4648-1056-5

Figure 1.10 Status of Implementation of EMIS Activities

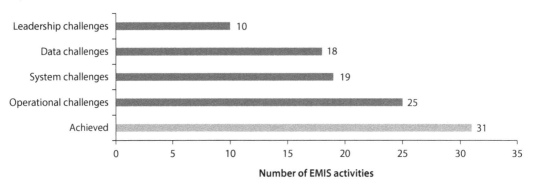

Figure 1.11 Categorization of Challenges

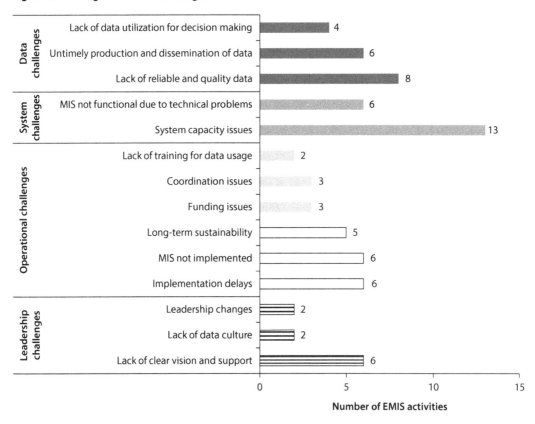

Note: MIS = Management Information System.

Notes

1. The maps displayed were produced by EdStats. The boundaries, colors, denominations, and any other information shown on this map do not imply, on the part of the World Bank Group, any judgment on the legal status of any territory, or any endorsement or acceptance of such boundaries. The maps are for reference only.

2. World Bank Education Statistics (EdStats).

3. The rest of the closed projects either did not have an ICR or there was not enough information on their performance to be able to comment on their status.

Lessons Learned from World Bank Education Management Information System Operations
http://dx.doi.org/10.1596/978-1-4648-1056-5

CHAPTER 2

Successes in EMIS Implementation

Establishing EMIS to Facilitate Information Sharing: The Case of Armenia

---

Box 2.1 Armenia: Education Financing and Management Reform Project (1998–2002)

Project Development Objective: The "strategic focus" of the project was (1) to facilitate improvements in the quality of general education by promoting school-level initiatives, by increasing opportunities and incentives for innovation throughout the system, and by improving the supply of textbooks and teaching materials, and (2) to help build the necessary institutional framework and capacity at all levels, for more efficient, equitable, and sustainable operation of the basic education system.

Education management information system (EMIS) Cost: Not specified (Project cost: $37.5 million)

EMIS Rating: Satisfactory

EMIS Objective: To (a) facilitate information sharing between regional and central level by establishing an EMIS, (b) monitor school statistics for planning purposes, and (c) improve monitoring of school performance and educational outputs.

Main Findings

Through the Armenia Education Financing and Management Reform Project (1998–2002), the country was able to establish an EMIS for the first time. The project was responsible for the collection, development, and analysis of general statistical data on the education system, at both the regional and country levels (box 2.1).

Data were collected using a single annual school questionnaire to provide information on, among other things, (a) student mobility data, (b) student achievement data (graduation exam marks and achievement scores), (c) quality of teaching staff (proportion of unqualified staff requiring in-service retraining),

Figure 2.1 Stages of Information Flow in Armenia

    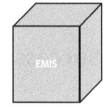

Stage 1: School	Stage 2: Regional government	Stage 3: EMIS center, Ministry of Education and science
Initial data collected at the school level (via school questionnaire): ✓ Students, teachers, nonteaching staff ✓ Assessment ✓ Instruction time ✓ Resources: infrastructure, budget, etc.	Information is summarized, edited, and corrected to get summative indicators used for accounting, planning, and management	

and (d) teacher distribution by age, subject, and qualification level. The establishment of an EMIS as the focal point of data storage resulted in improved coordination between different units of the government by streamlining the flow of information, eliminating duplication of efforts, and filling information gaps. Reliable and timely information was available, which helped in the utilization of data for policy decision making. The collection, analysis, and dissemination of information became a regular, annual process for the government (figure 2.1).

Key Takeaways
(a) Collection of comprehensive data, including student-level learning data to assess the education performance of the country and (b) a decentralized system with validation measures at the regional level to verify the quality of data entered into the EMIS.

EMIS in Fragile Contexts: The Case of Afghanistan

Box 2.2 Afghanistan: Education Quality Improvement Program (EQUIP) (2005–09)

Project Development Objective: To increase equitable access to quality basic education, especially for girls, through school grants, teacher training, and strengthened institutional capacity with support from communities and private providers.

   EMIS Cost: Not specified (Project cost: $460 million)

   EMIS Objective: To develop an EMIS and help build capacity of the Ministry of Education (MoE) officials for its effective use. The component was to support annual data collection from schools to promote the use of data in planning and decision making. It would also support MoE in undertaking a household survey to assess the status of schooling of children, direct and indirect cost of schooling, and any other opportunities and constraints concerning education.

Main Findings

Afghanistan is a perfect example of how an EMIS can be used to strengthen the monitoring systems in a country, even in fragile contexts. A heavy investment of $460 million was made into the EQUIP project in 2004 (box 2.2). When the project began, no sophisticated EMIS was in use in the country, and data were collected using paper-based census forms, which was unreliable and unsafe. With the growth of the education sector, and the support from young IT professionals, the government started to understand the power of data for decision making. Various technological initiatives were undertaken to collect and disseminate education data in a timely manner. The key achievement of the project was the development of multiple systems capturing education data: (a) Student Management System, (b) School Management System, (c) Human Resource Management System, (d) Geographical Information System (GIS), (e) Certificate Generation System, (f) Infrastructure Management System, and (g) Centrally Hosted Education Information System (at http://emis.af/index .aspx, figure 2.2).

Key Takeaways

(a) Improved accuracy through comprehensive electronic system of data collection, management, and analysis; (b) improved transparency through a single centralized Ministry portal to provide comprehensive data to all stakeholders; and (c) increased efficiency through the introduction of new technologies such as GIS and mobile applications to ensure data analysis happens in real time; and (d) improved local decision making as provinces manage their own data.

Figure 2.2 Snapshot of EMIS Data on the Afghanistan Government Website

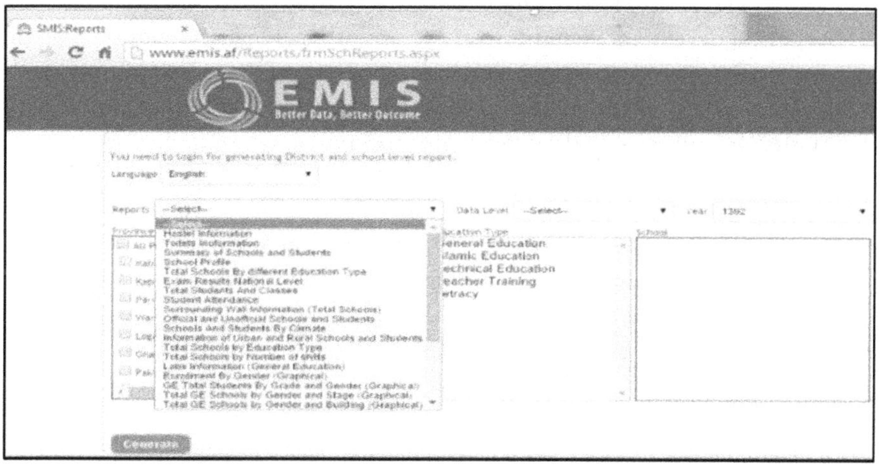

Source: EMIS Website (Ministry of Education, Afghanistan).

Lessons Learned from World Bank Education Management Information System Operations
http://dx.doi.org/10.1596/978-1-4648-1056-5

EMIS as a Management Tool: The Case of Bosnia and Herzegovina

---

Box 2.3 Bosnia and Herzegovina: Education Development Project (2000–05)

Project Development Objective: The project had the following three broad objectives: (a) to mobilize the professional capacity of teachers to improve the teaching and learning processes in schools and as a result improve the quality of education being offered to primary school children in Bosnia and Herzegovina; (b) to promote the efficient and equitable use of scarce public resources for education in the country by providing public policy makers and decision makers with management tools and information necessary to measure inputs, outputs, and outcomes in the education system; and (c) to promote cooperation and coordination across the three main constituent groups in an effort to reduce inefficient resource use and build a professional basis for stakeholder dialogue in education throughout Bosnia and Herzegovina.

    EMIS Cost: $2 million (Project cost: $14.43 million)

    EMIS Rating: Satisfactory

    EMIS Objective: To finance the development of a country-wide EMIS to enable improved sector management and compatibility of information among the country's decentralized education systems. It was also to test the viability of a "per-student budgeting model" designed to promote increased efficiency and equity in education spending.

Main Findings

The main objective of the EMIS component was to develop and finance implementation of an EMIS in all regions in Bosnia and Herzegovina to promote increased efficiency in education funding through the "per-student budgeting" model (box 2.3). The successful outcomes of the project were the following:

- Identification, design, program testing, and distribution of an EMIS for primary and secondary schools and ministries
- Successful development and delivery of professional management training on information systems to school directors, school accountants, and Ministry staff
- Creation of an electronic-based information system that is compatible with the structure of the country's education sector
- Expansion of the financial module to undertake efficiency analyses based on per pupil costs
- Enabling of all key stakeholders to effectively use the information system tools for education performance, monitoring, resource allocation, and accountability reporting
- Provide web-based access to the EMIS data for sector stakeholders.

Key Takeaways

(a) Developing a web-based system to avoid the delays in manual processing of information, (b) creating a web page to make EMIS data open to stakeholders, and (c) providing trainings to schools and Ministry staff to strengthen local capacity.

Creation of a Digital Platform to Access EMIS Data: The Case of Guatemala

---

Box 2.4 Guatemala: Universalization of Basic Education Project (2001–09)

Project Development Objective: The project had the following development objectives: (a) improve coverage and equity at the primary school level through the expansion and consolidation of PRONADE schools (National Community-Managed Program for Education Development) and by providing scholarships for indigenous girls in rural communities; (b) improve the efficiency and quality of primary education by supporting bilingual education, providing textbooks and didactic materials in 18 linguistic areas, expanding multigrade schools, and improving teachers' qualifications; (c) facilitate the joint design and execution between Ministry of Education and the Ministry of Culture and Sports of a program to enhance the goals of cultural diversity and pluralism contained in the National Constitution, the Guatemalan Peace Accords, and the April 2000 National Congress on Cultural Policies; and (d) assist the decentralization and modernization of Ministry of Education by supporting the ongoing efforts to strengthen the organization and management of the education system.

    EMIS Cost: Not specified (Project cost: $87.24 million)

    EMIS Rating: Not available

    EMIS Objective: The component supported the continued development and updating of an EMIS. The main objective was to upgrade the EMIS and use the new applications and technology as a tool for uniform educational monitoring, feedback, reporting, and decision making by departments.

Main Findings

The Universalization of Basic Education project (2001–09) supported the improvement of the EMIS in Guatemala through the use of enhanced technology (box 2.4). By project completion, significant improvements had been made in the quality of data entered in the system, in the decentralization of data collection and management, and in the availability and use of education data generated by the system, using the Ministry of Education's website. The Information and Automation System, at both the central and departmental levels, was strengthened through the Internet. A comprehensive Human Resources Information System was developed and implemented that contained 10 modules: posting management and wages, recruitment and selection, controls of personnel actions, disciplinary files, salary scales, training, performance evaluation, and integration of the list system.

The Guatemala Ministry of Education site is easily accessible and provides quick access to data that can be downloaded in Excel and HTML formats. The data include population disaggregated by age, enrollments by age/grade, and enrollment rates. The data are also sorted by regions,

Lessons Learned from World Bank Education Management Information System Operations
http://dx.doi.org/10.1596/978-1-4648-1056-5

departments, and municipalities. The website is a real-world example of a system that is easy to use and understand (Cassidy 2006).

Key Takeaways
(a) Easy access of data to education stakeholders and (b) use of technology to increase capacity of the system.

Strengthening and Expansion of EMIS to an Online System: The Case of Honduras

---

Box 2.5 Honduras: Education Quality, Governance, and Institutional Strengthening Project (2006–13)

Project Development Objective: To support the government of Honduras to increase the coverage, quality, accountability, and governance of its basic education system.

   EMIS Cost: Not specified (Project cost: $16.29 million)

   EMIS Rating: Satisfactory

   EMIS Objective: The component focused on strengthening the Ministry of Education through development and expansion of a web-based technological platform that contains information on education sector performance at all levels of the system. It also focused on expanding, strengthening, updating, and integrating information at central and subnational levels to allow for improved decision making and performance monitoring.

Main Findings
Through the Honduras Education Quality, Governance and Institutional Strengthening Project (2006–13), the country upgraded and strengthened the existing EMIS system to produce reliable educational statistics (box 2.5). The main achievements included the following:

- Timely collection of information on schools, teachers, and enrollment
- Historical education data was checked for consistency, reestimated for precision, and loaded into the system, including a diagnostic census of all schools located in Afro-Honduran and indigenous areas
- Computer equipment was provided at the central and departmental levels, along with the required training for staff at all levels
- All information was made available to the public to ensure transparency.

Key Takeaways
(a) Upgrading the existing system to a web-based platform to encourage effective utilization by all levels of government, and (b) providing training to enable them to use the software, and (c) giving open access to data (figure 2.3).

Figure 2.3　Factors That Led to Successful Implementation of EMIS in Honduras

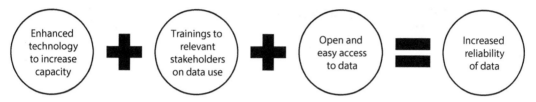

EMIS as a Tool to Strengthen Teaching and Learning: The Case of Lithuania

---

Box 2.6　Lithuania: Education Improvement Project (2002–07)

Project Development Objective: To improve student achievement in basic education (grades 5–10) and to make a more efficient use of the financial, human, and physical resources allocated to education, by supporting municipalities in their effort to optimize their school network, and by improving energy efficiency and space utilization in an initial group of 62 targeted schools.

　　EMIS cost: $1.5 million (Project cost: $64.89 million)

　　EMIS Rating: Not available

　　EMIS Objective: The component focused on strengthening the EMIS of the Ministry of Education and Sports to enhance the quality of teaching and learning in basic schools.

Main Findings

To monitor the education system more closely, the Education Improvement Project (2002–07) focused on strengthening the existing EMIS system in Lithuania (box 2.6). This included efforts to ensure timely collection data on system performance and utilization for decision making. It also generated interest among municipalities and school representatives, leading to the establishment of an EMIS at the local/municipal level and the school level (School Information Systems). The capacity of the Ministry of Education and Science was strengthened to provide timely system information and monitoring of education outcomes, to produce a National Education Report on an annual basis, to measure pupils' achievements, and to carry out school performance audits through the establishment of the National Audit Agency (figure 2.4).

Key Takeaways

(a) Developing an interest among local communities in using EMIS and (b) creating an annual education report to measure student achievement.

Figure 2.4 Snapshot of the EMIS Website at the Ministry of Education in Lithuania

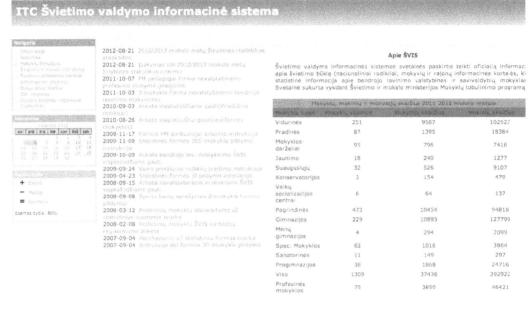

Source: Centre of Information Technology, Ministry of Education & Science, Lithuania.

Expansion of EMIS to Remote Schools: The Case of Malaysia

Box 2.7 Malaysia: Education Sector Support Project (1999–2005)

Project Development Objective: The overall objective was to assist the Borrower in (a) mitigating the adverse impact of the regional economic crisis on its education sector and (b) supporting its medium-term economic recovery by developing and enhancing student technical skills.

EMIS Cost: $9 million (Project cost: $244 million)

EMIS Rating: Highly Satisfactory

EMIS Objective: To improve the borrower's existing EMIS and expand its usage, especially in the states of Sabah and Sarawak.

Main Findings

This project in Malaysia on Education Sector Support (1999–2005) was successful in upgrading and expanding the existing EMIS (box 2.7). Equipment, computers, software, and furniture were provided to several targeted departments and divisions at the Ministry of Education (MoE) and selected schools, especially in the regions of Sabah and Sarawak, for the EMIS. In addition, technical assistance was provided in developing the systems and creating training programs for staff. The main achievements of the program were (a) sustaining and improving the already established EMIS; (b) ensuring that the EMIS is implemented nationally, with particular emphasis on reaching remote schools in the states of Sabah and

Figure 2.5 Example of a Malaysian School System's Interface

Source: Yahya and Chong, n.d.; Department of Management Science and System, Malaysia.

Sarawak, which were outside the MoE's computerized data management system; (c) facilitating the EMIS transition to a Y2K-compliant system by phasing out obsolete equipment and operating systems; and (d) building institutional capacity through integration of multiple databases and development of an Executive Information System (EIS) for planning and policy formulation (figure 2.5).

Key Takeaways
(a) Expansion of EMIS to schools, (b) complementing the creation of an EMIS with regular trainings, and (c) building capacity through integration of existing databases.

EMIS as a Planning Tool: The Case of Nigeria

Box 2.8 Nigeria: Second Primary Education Project (2000–04)

Project Development Objective: The objectives of the Second Primary Education Project (PEPII) were to assist the Borrower in (1) strengthening the human resource capacity in its primary schools, (2) creating an environment conducive to effective teaching and learning in its primary schools, (3) improving the quality and availability of curriculum and other instructional materials in the primary schools, (4) developing an enhanced information base to facilitate decision making, and (5) increasing national awareness about HIV/AIDS.

 EMIS Cost: Not specified (Project cost: $61.11 million)

 EMIS Rating: Satisfactory

 EMIS Objective: To develop a comprehensive information base for decision making and for planning and monitoring of the Universal Basic Education (UBE) program.

Lessons Learned from World Bank Education Management Information System Operations
http://dx.doi.org/10.1596/978-1-4648-1056-5

Main Findings

The project in Nigeria was successful in setting up a comprehensive education information system (box 2.8). Key output deliverables were the following: (a) School statistics were made available: national education statistics reports for 1996–2001 (baseline data) and 2003 (school census) were produced and distributed. These are being used in Education for All (EFA) and Universal Basic Education (UBE) state planning exercises and for wider policy discussion. (b) EMIS equipment and staff capacities were upgraded to manage national data collection, analysis, reporting, and dissemination of data. (c) Capacity was increased within the federal and state education ministries to translate and analyze raw school data into useable form. (d) Data collection and processing for all schools was institutionalized (to be carried out in February of every year). The production and distribution of these statistics reestablished a credible education data system. Education data collection, processing, and publishing improved. (e) Computers and computer accessories were procured for use.

Key Takeaways

(a) Institutionalization of data collection process (see figure 2.6), (b) regular production of data, (c) increased capacity at the state and federal ministries, and (d) utilization of data for planning and policy making.

See table 2.1 for a summary of success stories in EMIS implementation.

Figure 2.6 Data Collection Process in Nigeria

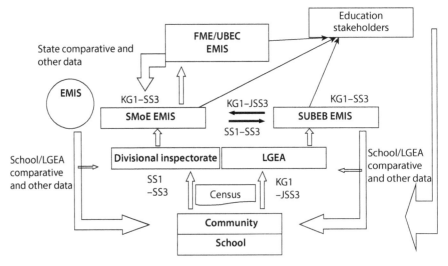

Source: World Bank 2005e Nigeria Second Primary Education Project.
Note: EMIS = Education Management Information System; FME = Federal Ministry of Education; JSS = junior secondary school; KG = kindergarten; LGEA = Local Government Education Agency; SMoE = State Ministries of Education; SS = senior secondary; SUBEB = State Universal Basic Education Board; UBEC = Universal Basic Education Commission.

Table 2.1 Summary of the Success Stories in EMIS Implementation

Afghanistan

Political buy-in from the government to establish EMIS to monitor education performance

Development of multiple systems to capture EMIS data

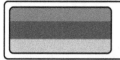

Armenia

Comprehensive school questionnaire to capture student data

Improved quality of data through validation measures at subnational level

Bosnia and Herzegovina

Establishment of a digital EMIS around the country

Efficiency analysis in policy formulation

Guatemala

Quality of data entered and decentralization of data collection

Accessibility of data from Ministry's website

Honduras

Web-based system to collect education data

Easy and open access to data

Trainings to relevant stakeholders for utilization of data

Lithuania

Development of political interest at schools and municipal level

Production of an annual yearbook with educational data

Malaysia

Expanding EMIS to remote schools

Capacity building through integration of databases

Nigeria

Institutionalization of data collection process

Data utilized to make policy decisions

CHAPTER 3

Challenges in EMIS Implementation

Leadership Challenges

Clarity was lacking among decision makers on the clear definition of an Education Management Information System (EMIS). Policy makers did not clearly understand its use and overall objective. No agreement was found on whether the EMIS aimed to collect and report statistical data to guide informed policy making, or alternatively, if it was simply a system to store information. For most countries, the lack of a clear definition was partly related to the large number of complex departments involved in the process—for example, education, planning and finance, science and technology, facilities—without any one entity assuming a strong leadership role. Often a lack of political buy-in was also found, which made EMIS implementation unsuccessful. In some cases, the lack of clarity about the EMIS stemmed from the lack of a data-driven culture. Leadership challenges can be further categorized into two areas:

- Unclear vision and limited buy-in
- Absence of institutionalization

Ten projects faced this issue: Albania, Argentina, Bulgaria, Bolivia, Colombia, India, the former Yugoslav Republic of Macedonia, Serbia, Sierra Leone, and Vietnam.

Unclear Vision and Limited Buy-In
Lack of strong leadership and clear vision on the functioning and objective of EMIS can be a deterrent to the success of an EMIS. A well-functioning EMIS needs strong leaders who have a clear understanding of its function and uses and are able to get support from various education stakeholders and other vested interests to build consensus and ultimately drive the EMIS forward.

Albania

Box 3.1 Albania: An Education Sector Project (2000–05)

Project Development Objective: To assist the Ministry of Education and Sciences (MoES) in planning and managing the delivery of educational services and strengthening its accountability to stakeholders for that delivery.

    EMIS Cost: $0.72 million (Project cost: $14.88 million)

    EMIS Rating: Unsatisfactory

    EMIS Objectives: To support a management information system that would link all branches of the Ministry, including district offices and universities. The key outputs were (a) a simple EMIS that could be easily extended in terms of data, applications, and users, introduced and tested in at least two pilot education district offices, and routinely used by policy makers and managers at Ministerial and district levels and (b) publication of the first Statistical Report Card on Albanian Education (SRCAE) for stakeholders.

Main Findings. In Albania, one of the key limitations of the project was that there was no clarity among the decision makers on how an EMIS should be used, that is, whether it should collect student-based information (to monitor participation and student performance) or school-based information (to monitor supplies and efficiency). The lack of clarity also stemmed from the fact that the key strategic and policy documents, which would have been able to identify the key information necessary to monitor, were developed during the last third of the project implementation period (box 3.1).

Although the project developed the fundamentals necessary for a functioning EMIS, including the development of a data collection and query system and both general administrative and analytical software, these systems and software never worked adequately. They were supposed to link the Ministry with two pilot school districts, but the link did not become functional, and data have not been collected or analyzed.

One positive measure is the statistical report card, which was first issued in 2004. The report is helpful for policy makers and the public alike and is published on a yearly basis. Also, a contact point was established in the Ministry for the public to be able to access information about the education sector; however, this facility is rarely used, and the data are somewhat outdated.

Key Takeaways. (a) There is a need for a strong leadership with clearly defined goals and objectives from the start of the project and (b) all concerned units should understand the vision and work together to avoid implementation issues.

Bulgaria

Box 3.2 Bulgaria: Education Modernization Project (2000–04)

Project Development Objective: The project objective is to (1) strengthen Ministry of Education and Science (MES) management and technical capacity for modernizing the sector; (2) increase MES capacity for introducing the new education standards and standards-based curriculum in general education, and for collecting and utilizing education information for monitoring and decision making in both general and higher education; (3) provide initial training to inspectors, school directors, and teachers on the newly introduced standards and curriculum; (4) expand a pilot program aimed at giving school directors greater discretion on spending decisions in their schools; (5) develop a methodology to support local efforts to optimize the school network; (6) reform the allocation process for resources and seats in higher education; (7) create a competitive fund for improving teaching, resource management, and internal quality assurance in higher education institutions; and (8) establish a modem student loan and stipend program for higher education.

EMIS Cost: Not specified (Project cost: $6.05 million)

EMIS Rating: Unsatisfactory.

EMIS Objective: This project involved setting up of two EMISs under two separate components: the General Education Management Information System (GEMIS) at the Ministry of Science and Education (MES) for the secondary level and the Higher Education Management Information System (HEMIS). The objectives of both EMISs were similar: (a) create and equip a unit for establishing and managing the information system, (b) design and validate data collection instruments and processes, and (c) train personnel to build capacity for analyzing and registering data.

Main Findings. In Bulgaria, neither of two proposed EMIS systems—the General Education Management Information System (GEMIS) and the Higher Education Management Information System (HEMIS)—was developed during the lifetime of the project. One of the main reasons was the lack of effective demand for information and policy formulation, performance monitoring, and decision making by the political leaders and senior officials at the Ministry. Although the process of collecting core statistics had begun by the end of the project, a tremendous gap existed between collection of education system statistics and establishment of the information systems (box 3.2).

Key Takeaways. (a) Information gathering, analysis, and dissemination is essential not only for the successful implementation of the project but also for the sustainability of an overall education reform, and (b) implementation of a fully operational EMIS requires political will to involve all related parties and stakeholders. Obtaining this political will is a key step in project design.

Lessons Learned from World Bank Education Management Information System Operations
http://dx.doi.org/10.1596/978-1-4648-1056-5

Vietnam

Box 3.3 Vietnam: Second Higher Education Project (2007–12)

Project Development Objective: To increase the quality of teaching and research in universities, in ways to improve the employability of graduates and the relevance of research.
　　EMIS Cost: Not specified (Project cost: $63.4 million)
　　EMIS Rating: Unsatisfactory
　　EMIS Objective: To build a Higher Education Management and Policy Information System (HEMPIS) using a set of standard key indicators to enable decision makers to monitor the performance of the higher education sector.

Main Findings. In Vietnam, the development of the Higher Education Management and Policy Information System (HEMPIS) proved to be more difficult than anticipated and was eventually canceled. Among the factors that contributed to its failed implementation was the lack of a clear definition regarding its overall objective. Specifically, no agreement was found on whether it was aimed at compiling and reporting statistical data or, alternatively, if it was going to serve as a more ambitious management tool.

The lack of a clear definition was partly related to the large number and diverse nature of the Ministry of Education and Training (MoET) departments involved in the process—for example, higher education, planning and finance, science and technology, facilities, international training and testing, and accreditation—without any one entity assuming a strong leadership role. Moreover, roughly four hundred higher education institutions that were expected to feed data to HEMPIS, most of which already have their own MIS in place, were not involved in the process (box 3.3).

Key Takeaways. (a) The objective for setting up an EMIS should be made clear before the start of the project, and (b) key stakeholders should be involved at early stages of EMIS development to incorporate their recommendations.

Absence of Institutionalization

Absence of EMIS specific policies along with continuous changes in the top management can impair the long-term sustainability of EMIS. A strong data governance committee, assembled with representation from all stakeholder groups and educational agencies, is essential to provide leadership and vision to the project. Continuous changes in leadership can impair this vision and make it difficult to implement the system.

Argentina

Box 3.4 Argentina: Rural Education Improvement (PROMER) Project (2006–14)

Project's Development Objective: To support national government policy to (1) improve the coverage, efficiency, and quality of the Argentine education system and (2) improve the governance of the education system through strengthening of the normative, planning, information, monitoring, and evaluation capacity at the national and provincial levels.

   EMIS Cost: $2.95 million (Project cost: $150 million)

   EMIS Rating: Moderately Satisfactory

   EMIS Objective: This component supported the development and implementation of a system of data collection, analysis, dissemination, and use of information for policy decisions at the national, provincial, and school levels. This broadly involved financing technical assistance and equipment (computers and software) for the system.

Main Findings. Argentina faced difficulties in developing an EMIS as a result of multiple leadership changes, which affected the implementation of the system. The National Directorate of Information and Educational Quality Evaluation (NDIEQE) underwent four leadership changes between 2005 and 2009. As a result, considerable delays were seen in the development of a data collection, analysis, and dissemination system and in providing technical assistance to the provinces on its effective use. This slowed down the entire project, because the success of any project and EMIS is dependent on effective leadership and a clear vision from the start of the project (box 3.4).

Key Takeaway. There is a need for a strong legal framework that supports a fully functional EMIS to avoid management and operational challenges due to changes in government leadership.

Bolivia

Box 3.5 Bolivia: Education Quality and Equity Strengthening Project (2000–07)

Project Development Objective: To increase the number of years of schooling completed (particularly at the primary level) and to improvement in the quality of that schooling. It will also develop approaches to reduce gender disparities in educational outcomes in selected municipalities where the differences are greatest.

   EMIS Cost: Not specified (Project cost: $125.3 million)

   EMIS Rating: Not specified

   EMIS Objective: To support and finance the existing EMIS, under the M&E component of the project. Throughout the project, Project activities were to support the development and dissemination of relevant descriptive statistics related to indicators and outcomes in the education sector at the national, departmental, and municipal levels.

Main Findings. In Bolivia, continual changes in leadership led to the failure of the project. During the initial years of the project implementation, the Ministry was able to use the EMIS to produce good quality education statistics in a timely fashion, disaggregated by gender, grade, geographic area, and the like. This information was also made publicly available at the Ministry of Education website. However, the last years of project implementation experienced changes in leadership and vision, and as a result, the information systems were neglected. Very little investment was made in maintaining the systems, and the quality of information became weak. Moreover, significant gaps occurred in delivery of information, all of which seriously impacted the long-term sustainability of the project (box 3.5).

Key Takeaway. There is a need for a strong legal framework that supports a fully functional EMIS to avoid management and operational challenges due to changes in government leadership.

Latvia

Box 3.6 Latvia: Education Improvement Project (1999–2005)

Project Development Objective: To improve energy efficiency and space utilization of educational facilities and to build and strengthen institutional management capacity to assess and promote quality learning. The goal of the project was to increase capacity within the Latvian education sector for continuous improvement of education outcomes by strengthening the management of both resource and inputs and the learning process.

   EMIS Cost: $0.53 million (Project cost: $39.76 million)

   EMIS Rating: Not specified

   EMIS Objective: To assess the Latvian EMIS, review the roles and responsibilities of the Ministry of Education and Science (MES) Policy Department, and develop a proposal for its effective implementation.

Main Findings. One of the significant weakness of the project was the insufficient integration of various management information systems into the Ministry of Education. This was extremely important to ensure the long-term sustainability of the system. The report also highlighted that the lack of integration could be due to the result of continuous changes in the top level of the Ministry, affecting the continuity of the projects and lack of a well-defined vision (box 3.6).

Key Takeaway. Developing a sound and comprehensive information system requires strong political will and clear objectives.

Data Challenges

Availability of reliable and consistent data remained a concern for most projects. Countries placed too much emphasis on collecting data without focusing on reliability and applicability of the data. As a result, considerable inconsistencies were found in the data. Even when efforts were made to produce quality data, timeliness remained a serious issue. Considerable time lags occurred in the publication and dissemination of information, thereby reducing the utility of data for decision making. Major causes for the failure were the inability of the government to understand the definition of EMIS, its objectives, and its usefulness in decision making. Low technical capacity for data collection and analysis also made it difficult to produce quality data. Quality data issues could be further categorized into three areas:

- Unreliable and poor quality of data
- Untimely production and dissemination of data
- Limited use of data for decision making.

Eighteen projects faced this issue: Brazil, Chad, Colombia, Costa Rica, Côte d'Ivoire, Ghana, Honduras, India, Kenya, Kosovo, Lesotho, FYR Macedonia, Nigeria, Pakistan, Sierra Leone, St. Kitts and Nevis, Tanzania, and Uruguay.

Unreliable and Poor Quality of Data

Many countries faced problems relating to the quality of data produced by the EMIS. In most cases, countries collected fragmented data, without any reliability and applicability considerations. Moreover, considerable inconsistencies were found in the data produced. The following examples illustrate the problem.

India

Box 3.7 India: Rajasthan District Primary Education Project (1999–2005)

Project Development Objective: To ensure that all 6–11-year-old children in nine districts, especially from socially and economically disadvantaged groups, have access to a five-year primary education cycle of appropriate quality. It is expected to result in increased enrollments and community involvement in primary education, improved teacher performance, better capacity to manage the education system, greater learning, and higher completion rates of the primary cohort.

    EMIS Cost: Not specified (Project cost: $109 million)

    EMIS Rating: Moderately Satisfactory

    EMIS Objective: To put in place an effective EMIS (as a part of M&E) to improve state and district capacity to improve primary education.

Main Findings. In Rajasthan, availability of reliable data remained a concern throughout the project. Too much data were collected without much emphasis on reliability and applicability. Considerable discrepancies and contradictions were found in the District Information System for Education (DISE) data because the size of the educational administration did not keep pace with the expansion of the school system (box 3.7). In addition to the DISE, the state initiated a baseline survey in 2001 and updated it in 2004 with a Child Tracking Survey (CTS). These data were not disaggregated based on specific groups of out-of-school children (e.g., children from families that migrate, transfers to private schools or to other districts/states, working children, urban deprived groups, and enrollment). Integration of the DISE data and the CTS did not take place, which would have been useful for effective planning. Data gathering and its management continued to remain an area of concern.

Along with the first project, the World Bank undertook another project in India called the "Rajasthan Second District Primary Education Project" (2001–08). The combined effort of the World Bank and the government of India (GOI) led to the development and strengthening of the EMIS, which became fully functional by the last year of the project. Now the data generated through DISE are increasingly being put to use by management. Efforts are still being made to integrate the DISE data and the CTS for effective planning and monitoring. The challenge, however, is to strengthen the culture and practice of using the EMIS as a management and planning tool, to continuously update the data and supplement it with additional survey-based information to help education planning.

Key Takeaway. Collection of education data should be linked with the overall national education goals. This would ensure more effective utilization of data, and the analysis of data would be useful for evaluating the overall performance of the education system.

Pakistan

Box 3.8 Pakistan: Northern Education Project (1998–2004)

Project Development Objective: To support the program for the development of the elementary school sector in Azad Jammu and Kashmir (AJK) and Northern Areas (NA) and, to that end, to assist in (a) improving the quality of education, (b) increasing equitable access to education, (c) strengthening institutional capacity, and (d) promoting community participation. NEP was designed to cover education from Katchi (kindergarten) to grade 8, with particular emphasis on the primary years and girls' education.

    EMIS Cost: Not specified (Project cost: $31.89 million)

    EMIS Rating: Not specified

---

box continues next page

Box 3.8: Pakistan: Northern Education Project (1998–2004) *(continued)*

EMIS Objective: To develop a reasonably effective and systematic EMIS with increased use of its data by government departments and development partners, and increased capacity among staff to manage and regularly update the EMIS. It also focused on providing incentives for information reporting and use, and establishing an area-specific education information database.

Main Findings. In Pakistan, incomplete information and low capacity were serious issues. Although education statistics were produced annually by the department in charge during the course of the project, significant gaps in the databases remained, with incomplete reporting from some schools. Moreover, gender aggregation of some data was inadequate (e.g., gender details of School Management Committees). EMIS reports were not distributed to schools, which, as a result, were not aware of their progress against performance indicators or their status in relation to other schools in the area (box 3.8).

Some of the common issues raised were (a) use of outdated information from schools, (b) limited data verification at each level, (c) nonuniform consolidation and data entry of all school forms at the district EMIS, (d) lack of understanding of the value of available information, and (e) inadequate capacity to use EMIS data; when used, decisions are focused primarily on facility construction/expansion and textbook provision (Nayyar-Stone 2013).

Key Takeaways. (a) Well-established data quality control checks at education level are needed to maintain reliable data useful for decision making and (b) regular discussions should be held with stakeholders to revisit the statistics collected by EMIS.

Untimely Production and Dissemination of Data

One of the common problems faced by countries was that they were unable to produce education statistics/report cards on a regular basis. This resulted in untimely dissemination of data to education stakeholders, making it difficult to be used in decision making. The following case studies illustrate the problem.

Chad

Box 3.9 Chad: Education Sector Project (2003–12)

Project Development Objective: To (1) improve access and equity for primary education and (2) increase capacity in strategic management and curriculum development.

EMIS Cost: $3.22 million (Project cost: $107 million)

box continues next page

EMIS Rating: Moderately Satisfactory

EMIS Objective: The component focused on developing capacity at all levels of the Ministry of Education (MoE) to produce timely education statistical yearbook and key education indicators. This was to include technical assistance (TA), training/workshops, and provision of goods and equipment.

Main Findings. In this project, timely production of data remained a concern; delays in data production and incomplete information were recurrent issues in the sector, and the reliability of data was questionable (box 3.9). The Department of Planning was expected to produce national and regional statistics on an annual basis. However, the Education Statistical Yearbook was published with at least a one-year delay and had limited dissemination, which reduced the use of information in policy dialogue and in informing policy decisions. Consistency in indicators was further complicated as a result of the use of population projections based on the 1999 census, which was used until 2009, when a new census was conducted. These data problems were mainly due to low capacity issues at decentralized levels.

Currently a project is ongoing in Chad called the "Second Phase of the Education Sector Reform Project (2013–18)," with one of its subcomponents dedicated to overcoming the challenges of the previous project. The EMIS component of this project is included as a part of M&E and aims to identify and pilot improvements in the EMIS. It focuses on strengthening the Ministry's capacity in evidence-based decision making, using a hands-on approach and data collection to monitor project activities. The Key Performance Indicators (KPIs) include designing/upgrading tools and institutional mechanisms (including coordination across the numerous data producing departments across the Ministry) for collecting and using school-level data for human resource management, statistical, and overall planning purposes.

Key Takeaway. Local capacity should be increased to ensure production of timely data and its effective utilization.

Ghana

box continues next page

Box 3.10 Ghana: An Education Sector Project (2004–11) *(continued)*

EMIS Objective: To (1) build on the success of the IDA-supported Basic Education Sector Improvement Project (BESIP) that established EMIS in 10 regions and 26 districts and (2) to upgrade the EMIS application to provide reliable, relevant, and timely data. The intermediate indicator used to measure this was the percentage of targeted districts for which the EMIS is used to generate annual reports.

Main Findings. The Ministry of Education in Ghana was able to produce, compile, and generate the education statistics yearbook regularly. However, these data were not made available to the public. Lack of utilization of data was a major problem. The project team believed that, in the future, Ghana would need to enhance their EMIS to reflect the increasing role of private sector provision, distance learning, detailed information on disadvantaged groups, and tertiary education. It also suggested that the Ministry of Education make the education statistics readily available online in a more user-friendly format to all education stakeholders for accountability and decision making (box 3.10).

Key Takeaways. (a) It is necessary to build capacity and generate demand for EMIS data so that the data are used in policy making and (b) have a clearly outlined public dissemination strategy in place.

Kenya

Box 3.11 Kenya: Education Sector Project (2006–10)

Project Development Objective: To support the government's program to provide basic education and improve the quality of education for all children by 2010: (1) ensuring equity of access to basic education, (2) enhancing quality and learning achievement, (3) providing opportunities for further education and training, and (4) strengthening education sector management.

EMIS Cost: $7 million (Project cost: $1,084 million)

EMIS Rating: Not specified

EMIS Objective: To strengthen the Ministry of Education's EMIS and provide timely and reliable data. By the end of the project, EMIS capacity was strengthened, and coverage of EMIS also improved over time.

Main Findings. In Kenya, data production and dissemination issues remained a persistent problem. The data generated via the EMIS were made available with a long delay that undermined the data's usefulness; validity and reliability remained issues throughout the project. Further, data were highly inconsistent, leading to overestimations of enrollment increases over time.

Finally, some key indicators, such as the Net Enrollment Rate and regional and gender disparities, did not correspond to information from other sources, such as household surveys (box 3.11).

Key Takeaway. Sound administration and implementation are needed to ensure that lags between data collection and publication of statistics get reduced.

Lesotho

Box 3.12 Lesotho: Second Education Sector Development Project (1999–2003)

Project Development Objective: The project will focus on increasing access and equity at the primary school level to lay the foundation for achieving universal primary education (UPE) over the program period (1999–2011), and on improving the quality of primary and secondary education. Furthermore, the project will develop the policy and institutional frameworks for ECD, TVET, and nonformal education.

   EMIS Cost: Not specified (Project cost: $26.7 million)

   EMIS Rating: Moderately Satisfactory

   EMIS Objective: To upgrade the EMIS to enhance the capacity at both the school level and the central level to accurately collect school data with the help of the revised survey forms. The Planning Unit staff would receive training to assist them in analyzing the EMIS data and will learn how to use this data to inform the policy decision-making process.

Main Findings. Lesotho's Education Planning Unit (EPU) was able to set up basic EMIS activities: (a) basic infrastructure such as hardware, software, and database applications were installed and developed, and (b) critical school-level data were collected and continue to be collected annually. Staff at the central and district levels were trained in data collection and processing. The Ministry's capacity to process education statistics was enhanced, and training courses were taken by the staff in the EPU. It was successful in producing quality education statistics after several years of investment. However, production of statistics remained an issue: The production did not take place in a timely fashion. The EPU was not able to produce these statistics on a yearly basis, as initially planned (box 3.12).

Key Takeaways. (a) There is a need to plan ahead to produce data in a timely fashion to ensure no implementation issues and (b) there needs to be a strategy on how to use the data to inform policy dialogue and planning.

Limited Use of Data for Decision Making

One of the common problems faced by the countries was the inability of the government to use the available information and education statistics to inform policy choices. Even when an EMIS was effectively implemented, it was not used by education stakeholders (e.g., teachers, parents, policy makers) to inform progress by the schools/education system. This was often due to the lack of a data-driven culture in the country, a culture that prioritizes data as a fundamental element of operations for decision making, both inside and outside of the education system. Evidence of a data-driven culture includes efforts made by the government to promote the collection and utilization of data within and beyond the education system (e.g., national census or population statistics). This is essential for a well-functioning EMIS. Examples bellow illustrate how the absence of this culture could make an EMIS ineffective and redundant.

Azerbaijan

Box 3.13 Azerbaijan: Education Sector Development Project (2003–10)

Project Development Objective: The Project Development Objectives are (1) more effective teaching and improved learning results in general secondary schools (a) that receive new school libraries and (b) where teachers adopt improved teaching practices as a result of in-service training and (2) improved efficiency of spending in education.

EMIS Cost: $0.7 million (Project Cost: $22.61 million)

EMIS Rating: Not specified

EMIS Objective: To assist the MoE in establishing a comprehensive EMIS to help managers monitor the system, and develop policy and action plans based on accurate and timely information. This included designing and deploying an EMIS in the Ministry, linking it with the district education offices and other institutions integral to the implementation of education reforms.

Main Findings. Azerbaijan is an example of lacking a data-driven culture. Although the project has been successful in establishing a comprehensive EMIS with quality data, it has not been put to use.

Before the start of the project, the Ministry of Education (MoE) had the following deficiencies with regard to efficient operations and management of an EMIS: labor-intensive, slow for data aggregation, difficult for data analysis, time consuming, and limited information. The establishment of the EMIS and introduction of national assessments of student learning achievement provided adequate tools for the Ministry to strengthen capacity for planning and monitoring education reforms. An EMIS unit was established in the MoE and became fully operational. The EMIS database comprised information on general schools including comprehensive information on students and teachers, school principals and other staff, physical facilities, and the like. The EMIS Unit made publicly available a school-by-school database at the MoE official website. The Unit was also able to electronically receive and handle education statistics. Although the EMIS database was rich with information about general schools and is available on the MoE LAN, not many people used the EMIS. The main user of the EMIS was the M&E Unit of the MoE for purposes related to implementation of different types of assessments including exams and national and international assessments. The main reason for limited use of the EMIS was the lack of culture and skills to use the computerized information database (box 3.13).

Key Takeaways. (a) Efforts should be made to educate stakeholders across the education system on the importance of education data to make important policy decisions and (b) a data-driven culture prioritizes data as a fundamental element of operations and decision making, both inside and outside of the education system.

St. Kitts and Nevis

Box 3.14 St. Kitts and Nevis: Education Development Project (OECS) (2002–09)

Project Development Objective: To build human capital in the OECS, which, in turn, will contribute to the diversification of their economy and more sustainable growth. This objective will be achieved by (1) increasing access to secondary education, (2) improving the quality of the teaching and learning process, with more direct interventions at the school level and a focus on student-centered learning, and (3) strengthening management of the sector and governance of schools.

   EMIS Cost: $0.002 million (Project cost: $7.77 million)
   EMIS Rating: Moderately Satisfactory
   EMIS Objective: This component focused on upgrading the planning, management, and information processing capabilities of the education system through the expansion of an EMIS, including EMIS training.

Main Findings. In St. Kitts and Nevis, one major success area was the mainstreaming of the electronic tools in data collection. Availability of data was improved by establishing e-mail and Internet connections for all schools and designing school websites and simple instruments for data collection. Basic school data such as student enrollment and teacher employment were collected from schools on a timely basis, improving the time lag from more than two years in 2003 to less than a year in 2008. The statistical digest was published for the school year 2007/08, which contained key education data at all levels such as enrollment, Caribbean Examinations Council (CXC) Report, and number of trained teachers. However, data were not utilized systematically for implementation of activities (e.g., schools did not use the EMIS for making decisions). Based on the progress made on the data collection, but with a major shortfall in utilization of data and implementation of planned activities, the achievement of this objective is rated moderately unsatisfactory. In addition, there were other technical problems: The procurement of EMIS software was dropped because of high maintenance costs, which made it difficult to strengthen the system's capacity (box 3.14).

Key Takeaway. Data validation mechanisms to improve the quality of data will generate demand for data for making decisions.

Tanzania

Box 3.15 Tanzania: Secondary Education Development Program (2004–07)

Project Development Objective: To improve the quality of secondary education with a focus on underserved areas.

 EMIS Cost: Not specified (Project cost: $469.30 million)

 EMIS Rating: Not specified

 EMIS Objective: The component focused on the expansion of the EMIS to capture data on secondary education that are accurate, easy to retrieve and process, readily available to all, and useful for decision making and for ensuring transparency and efficiency.

Main Findings. In Tanzania, the Ministry of Education faced many challenges in developing and utilizing a robust EMIS, with weak data quality and verification processes. Analytical work was also underdeveloped, and the potential of the EMIS to facilitate informed planning and policy making within the Ministry was not sufficiently realized. Throughout the project, broader management reforms were undertaken to improve the quality of data available from the EMIS, which resulted in timely statistical information. However, the extent to which the data are being used for policy and decision making still needs to be strengthened, and efforts are being made to improve it (box 3.15).

Key Takeaway. There is a need to build a data-driven culture in the country to ensure sustainability of the system.

Operational Challenges

For most projects, a common concern was the long-term sustainability of the EMIS because of problems related to management, finance (especially after the World Bank funding was exhausted), and staffing. Some of the challenges included continuous changes in the management team, inadequate functioning of software and systems, incomplete data collection, and lack of staff trained at the local and national levels to understand the system. Thus, it is important to think of an EMIS as more than just an IT system and to create an enabling environment for the people and processes that are the essential operational elements of EMIS.

Twenty-three countries faced this issue: Albania, Bangladesh, Cape Verde, Chad, Republic of Congo, Costa Rica, Djibouti, the Gambia, India, Kenya, Lebanon, Maldives, Mozambique, Namibia, Nicaragua, Nigeria, Sierra Leone, St. Vincent and the Grenadines, St. Kitts and Nevis, Timor-Leste, Uganda, the West Bank and Gaza economy, and the Republic of Yemen.

Capacity and Coordination Issues

Operational issues such as a lack of coordination between different teams of the project, inadequate funding, and other implementation delays can impair and slow down the functioning of an EMIS, resulting in a complete breakdown of the system.

Hungary

Box 3.16 Hungary: Higher Education Reform Project (1998–2004)

Project Development Objective: To (a) increase responsiveness to social and economic needs, (b) improve the operating efficiency of the system, (c) mobilize private finance, and (d) improve equity in higher education finance.

   EMIS Cost: $1.09 million (Project cost: $7.29 million)

   EMIS Rating: Not specified

   EMIS Objective: Management Information Systems were to be supported through the development of new management information structures, procedures, and systems in the integrating higher education institutions. The project was to finance expert services for the development of strategy and process redesign, software development, upgrading of information technology networks, and training support.

Main Findings. Hungary faced many operational challenges in setting up a new EMIS throughout the implementation of the project. By project closing, there was no real outcome of the component because changes by the manager were continuous throughout the project. Moreover, significant coordination problems occurred between the Ministry of Education, the Higher Education Institutes, and suppliers, which made the execution of the project difficult. The project team ignored the hidden complexities of the information system and overestimated its performance ability, which led to a complete breakdown of the system (box 3.16).

Key Takeaways. (a) There is a need to understand the core function of the EMIS before the start of the project, and (b) there should be clarity on the technological aspects and buy-in from all vested interests.

Lebanon

Box 3.17 Lebanon: General Education Project (2000–09)

Project Development Objective: To support the government's efforts to (1) enhance the capacity of the Ministry of Education, Youth and Sports (MNEYS) to function as an effective manager of the education sector, and (2) restore the credibility of the public general education system through improvements in quality and efficiency as well as increased access at the basic and junior secondary levels.

  EMIS Cost: Not specified (Project cost: $43.2 million)

  EMIS Rating: Not specified

  EMIS Objective: The objective of the component was to launch an EMIS to support timely and documented decision making and develop a national education strategy. This included in particular (a) development of EMIS within the Ministry of Education and Higher Education (MEHE) and the establishment of the Information Management Unit (IMU) within MEHE and (b) provision of computer equipment for this task

---

Main Findings. Lebanon was successful in establishing an effective EMIS at the Ministry of Education and Higher Education (MEHE), together with an Information Management Unit (IMU) and a program of end-user training. A School Information System (SIS), linked to the EMIS, was in place to support information needs at the individual school level. Although these components were delivered, they were not fully operational for use by the Ministry (box 3.17). Some of the common issues that arose were the following:

- Operational issues: The SIS software package was developed, equipment was delivered to all schools in Lebanon, relevant staff were trained, but the SIS was operational in fewer than 10 percent of schools.
- Staffing issues: The project team came to realize that effective implementation of comprehensive EMIS/IT components required timely recruitment and continuity of a sufficient number of suitable staff at the Ministry to ensure outputs were delivered and fully operational by project closing and to ensure requisite internal capacity is developed in the Ministry.

Currently a World Bank project is ongoing in Lebanon, the Second Education Development program (2011–17), to continue with the efforts of MEHE on EMIS. This project is focusing on enhancing and consolidating an EMIS, GIS, academic portal, examination systems, and other systems. A key activity would be capacity building for MEHE staff (headquarters, regional offices, and schools) in the use of information for decision making and utilizing the EMIS. Furthermore, the school information system will be enhanced to include a school management platform to assist principals, teachers, and administrators in managing the educational processes at the regional and school levels.

Lessons Learned from World Bank Education Management Information System Operations
http://dx.doi.org/10.1596/978-1-4648-1056-5

Key Takeaway. An EMIS is beyond technology; regular investment needs to go into hiring quality EMIS staff and providing regular trainings to enhance their capacity.

St. Vincent and the Grenadines

Box 3.18 St. Vincent and the Grenadines: OECS Education Development Project (2004–12)

Project Development Objective: To (1) increase equitable access to secondary education; (2) improve the quality of the teaching and learning process, with more direct interventions and provision of resources at the school level, and a focus on student-centered learning and mechanisms to provide student support; and (3) strengthen management of the sector and governance of schools.

    EMIS Rating: Not specified

    EMIS Cost: Not specified (Project cost: $9.32 million)

    EMIS Objective: To strengthen the EMIS to make reliable information available to inform decision making. The strengthening of EMIS and the development of performance indicators was to be sustained through a staff position in the planning unit at the Ministry.

Main Findings. In St. Vincent and the Grenadines, one of the clearly delineated benchmarks for success of the project was the strengthening of the Ministry of Education's electronic management information system to improve data generation and monitoring and evaluation capabilities of the Ministry (box 3.18).

From 1999 to 2011, school-level and aggregate data were collected on enrollment and test performance and broken down by gender. This data collection allowed for tracking of school enrollment as well as test scores on Caribbean Examinations Council exams in aggregate and by gender. Improved school supervision by the education officers contributed to better monitoring and assessment of achievements at the school level. Training was also provided to school principals on the compilation and use of school- and sector-level data. However, the EMIS subcomponent had to be abandoned because the funds allocated were inadequate and the suitable alternative measures could not be implemented within the framework of the project.

Key Takeaway. There should be a separate budget set for establishing and maintaining EMIS to ensure continuity of operations.

Timor-Leste

Box 3.19 Timor-Leste: Education Sector Support Project (ESSP) (2007–13)

Project Development Objective: To strengthen the capacity of the Ministry of Education and Culture for effective policy development, resource management, and innovation.
    EMIS Cost: Not specified (Project cost: $20.3 million)
    EMIS Rating: Moderately Satisfactory
    EMIS Objective: To set up an EMIS to inform policy making. Through its support for the EMIS and for M&E, ESSP will develop an understanding of the status of education in Timor-Leste adequate to facilitate system and student performance monitoring.

Main Findings. In Timor-Leste, the EMIS was established and maintained with support of the Education Sector Support Project (ESSP) and other donors. Their joint efforts resulted in immense progress in development of the EMIS infrastructure and applications, online access to education data, system maintenance, and data collection, input, and initial processing. It has laid a basis for the introduction of evidence-based policy and planning, as well as the promotion of management by reporting. The current system provides the Ministry with an opportunity to measure progress in education sector development using basic indicators. It also resulted in regular production of Education Statistical Yearbooks (box 3.19).

However, because of the longer initial phase of EMIS establishment and inadequately coordinated donor support, capacity building in data analysis and consolidated reporting was to a large extent underdeveloped. No capacity is found as yet within the EMIS for exploitation of the database for analytical work and little for the Ministry of Education (MoE) to underpin policy making and budgetary allocation decisions based on the EMIS and learning outcomes findings. The findings of the nonstandardized annual national examination (a scheme operated by the MoE's Curriculum Directorate) are not articulated with the EMIS data or with the infrastructure information collected by the Infrastructure Facility Unit.

Key Takeaways. (a) There is a need to build capacity and generate demand for EMIS data so that they are used in policy making, and (b) coordinated donor efforts and sustained high-level support/political will are essential for a well-functioning EMIS.

Turkey

Box 3.20 Turkey: Basic Education Project (1999–2003)

Project Development Objective: The Basic Education Program is the government's action program to apply its new basic education strategy. The objectives of the strategy (and of

box continues next page

Box 3.20 Turkey: Basic Education Project (1999–2003) *(continued)*
the Program) are (1) to achieve universal coverage in an expanded, eight-year basic education cycle (formerly five years), (2) to improve the quality and relevance of basic education, and (3) to make basic education schools a learning resource for the community.

EMIS Cost: Not specified (Project cost: $286 million)

EMIS Rating: Unsatisfactory

EMIS Objective: To support the Ministry's Council for Research and Planning (APK) to improve the Ministry's educational information management capacity, train and strengthen APK technical staff in the use of education management information systems, and acquire up-to-date computer hardware and software.

Main Findings. Turkey was unsuccessful in establishing the planned EMIS under this project. At the provincial level, there was limited capacity building in terms of promoting and coordinating education work. Schools and communities were not able to actively participate in the plans, and eventually the World Bank and borrower agreed to drop the project (box 3.20).

Key Takeaway. There is a need to build capacity and generate demand for EMIS data so that they are used in policy making.

System and Technological Challenges

Designing an EMIS is a challenging task requiring financing to develop and implement a new information system at both local and national levels. For most projects, this has been a major challenge. At the local level, problems arose in installing the computer equipment and developing the software for an information system. In many cases, the technical specifications for the development of the software were not finalized. The effort lacked coordination and failed to make the specifications compatible with the existing information systems. In some cases, the procurement process for computer equipment failed. Even when software was developed for all levels of the education system and made available to all schools, the computerized student record system is used only partially.

Seventeen countries faced this issue: Afghanistan, Bangladesh, Chile, Costa Rica, the Dominican Republic, Georgia, Jordan, Kosovo, the Lao People's Democratic Republic, Lesotho, Mauritania, Sierra Leone, Turkey, Ukraine, Vietnam, the West Bank and Gaza economy, and Zambia.

Integration Issues

Developing the EMIS and expanding the capacity of the system can be a technologically challenging task. The systems and software need to be continuously updated to accommodate the ever-changing need for data. It is also important to ensure that information systems interact with one another to enable the integration of these systems into one comprehensive EMIS. Technical problems related to any of those mentioned above can impair the functioning of the systems. These problems referred to the complete breakdown or inability of an EMIS to function due to system capacity issues, software problems, integration issues, or lack of Internet/computers to make data available to public. The following examples illustrate these issues.

Eritrea

Box 3.21 Eritrea: Education Sector Improvement Project (2003–12)

Project Development Objective: To increase enrolment in basic education, particularly for disadvantaged children, while improving the quality of basic and secondary education. The government of Eritrea has committed to achieving the Millennium Development Goals, including completion of a full course of primary schooling for all children and gender equality at all levels, and the Project will assist in helping the government to establish a firm basis for full achievement of the MDGs.

    EMIS Cost: Not specified (Project cost: $47.6 million)

    EMIS Rating: Not specified

    EMIS Objective: To strengthen the EMIS through Geographic Information System (GIS) technology. The project purchased the technology to facilitate a school mapping exercise and collection of school-level data that could be used with the EMIS.

Main Findings. In Eritrea, data collected through the Geographic Information System (GIS) system were routinely used to produce statistical yearbooks to track progress. Furthermore, with the help of the GIS technology, the project kept a database with information about all schools in the country, including existing ones as well as those financed by donors during the life of the project, which allowed the government to make informed decisions about its school construction program. A separate EMIS was also developed for the entire education sector and is being used to compile the annual education statistics and to inform policy decisions. This was a remarkable achievement considering all of the exogenous factors that affected project implementation. However, the government and the project would have benefited from full integration of the two systems, which would have made tracking and reporting easier and improved the effectiveness of the M&E officer assigned to the activities (box 3.21).

Key Takeaways. (a) A multisystem approach to data management is problematic when databases are neither integrated nor compatible, and (b) technological standards regarding integration and compatibility are necessary to ensure sustainability and proper system use.

Mauritania

Box 3.22 Mauritania: Higher Education Project (2004–13)

Project Development Objective: To "help the Government of Mauritania to implement its strategy of producing qualified graduates with the skills needed for increased productivity and diversification of its economy." The project is designed to (1) improve the quality of the learning environment and the relevance of courses to the labor market and (2) establish pedagogic, administrative, and financial management systems in the Institute of Higher Education (IHEs).

    EMIS Cost: Not specified (Project cost: $6.6 million)

    EMIS Rating: Not specified

    EMIS Objective: To support the establishment of, and related training for, an integrated MIS. This system would include information on and tracking of admissions and scholarships, student records, financial management, and inventories for physical plants and equipment. It would also include a quality assurance system covering pedagogic, financial, and administrative functions.

Main Findings. An integrated EMIS for student services, finance, human resources, planning, and monitoring was not established in Mauritania though separate systems do exist; financial and accounting reports, student tracer study reports, and plan of operations based on the MIS were not produced and audited under the project. This project was more complex than initially thought. After several technical problems related to underestimating the complexity of the intended MIS, development of the integrated MIS is still ongoing. In the meantime, the university developed systems for financial, examination, and student flow management (box 3.22).

Key Takeaways. It is important to have a sound data architecture and plan for data integration during the early stages of the project.

Vietnam

Box 3.23 Vietnam: Primary Education for Disadvantaged Children Project (2003–11)

Project Development Objective: To improve access to primary school and the quality of education for disadvantaged girls and boys.

    EMIS Cost: Not specified (Project cost: 258 million)

    EMIS Rating: Not specified

    EMIS Objective: To harmonize district-level school data collection efforts with the national EMIS and carry out analytical studies to increase sector-wide effectiveness and efficiency.

Main Findings. The EMIS component of the project was designed in 2004 and improved through years of the project (box 3.23). The database covered all primary schools in Vietnam and included aggregated information on school-age population, schools, teachers, and students. Indicators and datasets were expanded and updated every year to include information such as disability, migration, and boarding schools. More logic checks were gradually added to avoid data entry mistakes. The most important outcome of the EMIS activity was the creation of a comprehensive EMIS for the primary education level. In addition, authorized school staff were provided with the necessary training on data collection. However, some implementation challenges were involved throughout the project: (a) The project required schools to complete paper forms, then Bureaus of Education and Training to fill in the form online, then the Ministry of Education and Technology (MoET) to conduct data analysis and reporting, which necessitated enormous training needs and costs; (b) issues arose with data accuracy due to paper-form entry; (c) some indicators/data were hard to collect, especially the ones related to disability; and (d) because of large implementation costs, the EMIS was abandoned because no source of funding is available to maintain the system.

Current Status. Recently Vietnam developed a new EMIS designed, at no cost, by a state-owned telecommunication corporation. This system covers all general education levels. Schools can fill in the forms online, and data immediately go to the Ministry for analysis. A similar system/component for tertiary education level has also been designed.

Key Takeaway. EMIS system design needs to be user-friendly so it is easy to work with and sustainable.

Lessons Learned from World Bank Education Management Information System Operations
http://dx.doi.org/10.1596/978-1-4648-1056-5

CHAPTER 4

Annual School Census and Statistical Handbooks

To ensure a well-functioning Education Management Information System (EMIS), regular collection of education data through the annual school census (ASC) is crucial. At the same time, collecting accurate, reliable, and annual data on education from schools is a challenging task. Many countries grapple with the difficulty of conducting the school census annually, which delays the data collection and dissemination process. Most of the projects related to EMIS development did not succeed because of lack of institutionalization of the school census exercise. Even when the school census was conducted, the scope and quality of statistics were not sufficient for use in decision making such as allocation of resources, management of schools, and policy making. Data collected are restricted to aggregate school-level administrative numbers such as teachers.

The examples below highlight the issue related to school census, which is very common is other countries as well.

Pakistan (Sindh): Education Sector Project (SEP) (P107300), 2009–12

The development objective of the proposed project was to increase school participation, reduce gender and rural-urban disparities, increase progression, and improve the measurement of student learning. To this end, one of the components focused on monitoring the EMIS system in Sindh through improvements in the ASC conducted to collect data from schools.

Annual School Census: This is an annual census of all government schools and is the government's primary school facility survey. It captures basic information on school characteristics, enrollment by grade and gender, and teacher-level information. Information for the ASC forms are expected to obtained via observation at school (e.g., such as the state of school infrastructure and amenities), interviews with or self-completion by the school head or teachers (such as detailed information on teaching staff), or recording from information in school registers (such as student enrollment on the reference date).

Given the importance of this tool for effective evidence-based decision making, improvements in the reliability and timeliness of data generated through ASC was key. As such, the World Bank support included (1) the use of standardized processes (for field data collection, entry, verification, and validation), (2) further improvements in the scope of information collected, (3) stronger internal and external controls on data quality, (4) improved dissemination, (5) capacity building of provincial and district staff in data management, analysis, and utilization, and (6) provision of equipment.

However, by the end of the project, issues were still present with the quality of data generated by EMIS. The World Bank team felt that the poor achievement on the statistics was very likely the result of estimating this statistic from administrative data whose reliability and quality at baseline is highly questionable.

Republic of Congo: Support to Basic Education Project (P084317), 2004–13

The development objective of the project was to improve efficiency in the allocation and management of resources, improve the quality of education services offered, and reduce inequities in the provision of the services. To this end, one of the components focused on supporting the establishment and operationalization of an EMIS at the central and regional levels that could facilitate the development of coherent and efficient education sector programs. The Project, therefore, planned to (1) support capacity building of planning units at the central and regional levels; (2) procure the necessary physical inputs for the planning units to function, including computers and software, energy generators, and office equipment; and (3) pilot and implement yearly data collection and analysis and produce education statistics yearbooks.

To implement annual data collection process to produce school yearbooks, the Project financed and provided technical assistance to conduct a school census. Baseline data on the sector and on the basic education school network were collected. In addition, questionnaires were prepared and piloted for regular data collection on the key indicators. In addition to supporting data collection activities, the project also supported data cleaning and analysis and production of school yearbooks. The school mapping method was also introduced in several regions of the country, which allowed for the preparation of manuals defining the roles of each administrative level. Finally, the data collected allowed for the preparation of an education sector country status report. However, the full rollout of the EMIS was not accomplished during the project life because the annual production of statistics was carried out with significant delays. Coordination challenges are still found in terms of preparing for data collection, ensuring adequate funding, undertaking data analysis, and producing annual yearbooks on time.

Ghana: Basic Education Sector Improvement Project (P000975), 1997–2001

The project was designed to support the government of Ghana (GOG) in implementing its policy to achieve free, compulsory, and universal basic education (FCUBE). The EMIS in Ghana was a source of progress for management efficiency. The senior education officials have been sensitized about the importance of the data in management, which was reflected in the Educator Sector Plan (ESP) for which the EMIS will be further developed to serve as a tool for monitoring and evaluation. As such, the project focused on developing the EMIS to support policy analysis and planning, the management review process, and monitoring program targets and standards.

By the end of the project, the following milestones were achieved:

- Establishment of EMIS sites in 10 regions and 26 districts with training provided to the EMIS staff who are able to perform basic data management and data analysis
- Generation of five years of ASC data from 1997 to 2001 in a timely manner
- Production of the key education indicators and of policy-relevant data analysis
- Sensitization of education officials in the use of data for planning and decision making.

This was significant given that no systematic annual census using an EMIS had taken place in the country. However, a few outstanding issues still remained: (1) the school census still did not cover all levels of education (e.g., tertiary, vocational/technical, and nonformal education data were not captured); (2) the EMIS software application design was lacking, which led to limited data retrieval capability and user-unfriendly interface (e.g., users cannot easily retrieve data without EMIS unit staff's help); and (3) financial sustainability was an issue: the EMIS staff were still unable to develop the EMIS application independently and had to rely on outside help.

The Annual Census form in Ghana has been revised to include education data on enrollment and number of schools disaggregated into public and private by region and district. It also has information on teachers by sex and whether they are trained or untrained. Data on conditions of classrooms and other infrastructural conditions of the school are also captured (figure 4.1).

Lessons Learned from World Bank Education Management Information System Operations
http://dx.doi.org/10.1596/978-1-4648-1056-5

Figure 4.1 Snapshot of the Annual School Census Survey (2012–13) in Ghana

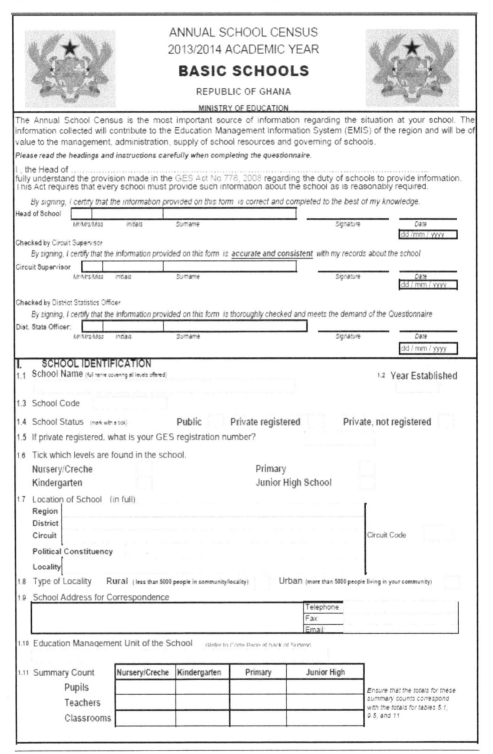

figure continues next page

Figure 4.1 Snapshot of the Annual School Census Survey (2012–13) in Ghana *(continued)*

2 SCHOOL PROFILE AND ORGANISATION

2.1 Indicate <u>NUMBER</u> of classes which are Multigrade by level

KG ☐
PRIM ☐
JHS ☐

Multigrade = These are classes where the same teacher teaches pupils in different grades in one classroom, e.g. pupils in grade 1 and grade 2 are taught in the same classroom.

2.2 Which of these levels run shift system in your school?

KG ☐
PRIM ☐
JHS ☐

These are schools where there are not enough classrooms to accommodate all pupils. The school day is divided into two sessions where the two groups of pupils are under same head or different heads.

2.3 Is your school one of two <u>DIFFERENT</u> schools making use of the same building? Yes ☐ No ☐

2.4 If YES, what is the name of the other school you are sharing with?

2.5 Is your school ? Boys only ☐ Girls only ☐ Co-educational/mixed ☐

2.6 Is your school a Special Education School? (see definition in manual) Yes ☐ No ☐

2.7 Indicate <u>NUMBER</u> of physically challenged pupils by level whether or not your school is a Special School.

	Impairement			Challenges	
	Blind / Visual	Hearing & Speech	Blind & Hearing	Physically Challenged	Intellectually Challenged
KG					
Primary					
JHS					

2.8 Does your school have Ramps for physically challenged pupils? Yes ☐ No ☐

2.9 What type of Support do you need for your physically challenged pupils? (Tick as applicable)

Ramps ☐ Hearing Aids ☐ Reading Glasses ☐ Wheel Chairs ☐ Braille ☐ Other ☐

2.10 What Ghanaian language(s) are taught in your school? (Mark with a tick)

Asante ☐ Dagbani ☐ Ewe ☐ Ga ☐ Kasem ☐ Wale/Dagaare ☐
Akwapem ☐ Dangme ☐ Fante ☐ Gonja ☐ Nzema ☐ Other ☐

2.11 How far away from the school is ... ?

A. the district education office Less than 5kms ☐ 5 - 10kms ☐ 11 -15kms ☐ More than 15kms ☐

B. the Head's house Less than 1kms ☐ 1 - 5kms ☐ 6 -10kms ☐ More than 11kms ☐

C. the next primary school Less than 5kms ☐ 5 - 10kms ☐ 11 -15kms ☐ More than 15kms ☐

3 SCHOOL INFRASTRUCTURE

3.1 Can a vehicle access your school? Yes ☐ No ☐

3.2 If YES, what is the road made of? (Tick one box) Tar ☐ Earth ☐ Gravel ☐

3.3 Does your school own a safe water facility? Yes ☐ No ☐

3.4 What type of safe water facility is available? (Tick one box) Pipe borne water ☐ Borehole ☐ Well ☐ Other ☐

3.5 What is the MAIN water storage facility available in the school? (Tick one) Tank ☐ Buckets/Pots ☐ None ☐ Other ☐

3.6 Is your school wired for electricity ? Yes ☐ No ☐

3.7 If YES, is it functional? Yes ☐ No ☐ N/A ☐

3.8 Is your community on electricity? Yes ☐ No ☐

3.9 If YES, please specify. National Grid ☐ Local Generator ☐ Other ☐ N/A ☐

3.10 How MANY individual toilet seats are available? Boys ☐ Girls ☐

3.11 How MANY individual toilet seats are functional? Boys ☐ Girls ☐

3.12 Are urinals available and functional? Yes ☐ No ☐

3.13 Which of these problems are experienced in your school?. (Tick box only if answer is yes)

Drainage blockages ☐ Soil erosion ☐ Waste water and sewage ☐ Garbage disposal ☐ Other ☐

figure continues next page

Lessons Learned from World Bank Education Management Information System Operations
http://dx.doi.org/10.1596/978-1-4648-1056-5

Figure 4.1 Snapshot of the Annual School Census Survey (2012–13) in Ghana *(continued)*

7 PUPILS AND TEACHER TEXTBOOKS

7.1 Indicate the NUMBER of Teaching Guides / HandBooks available by grade

	KG 1	KG 2	P1	P2	P3	P4	P5	P6	JH1	JH2	JH3
English											
Mathematics											
Environmental Studies											
Creative Activities/Arts											
Physical Education											
Natural / Integrated Science											
Music & Dance											
ICT											
Psycho social Studies/ RME											
Ghanaian Language/ Language Literacy											
Citizenship Education											
Social Studies											
French											
Basic Design & Tech											
Special Educ Only*											
Audio Therapy*											
Speech Therapy*											

7.2 How MANY Pupil Textbooks for each subject and grade is available ? (Indicate NIL if none are available)

	KG 1	KG 2	P1	P2	P3	P4	P5	P6	JH1	JH2	JH3
English											
Mathematics											
Environmental Studies											
Creative Activities/Arts											
Physical Education											
Natural / Integrated Science											
Music & Dance											
ICT											
Psycho Social Studies / RME											
Ghanaian Language/ Language Literacy											
Citizenship Education											
Social Studies											
French											
Basic Design & Tech											
Special Educ Only*											
Audio Therapy*											
Speech Therapy*											

figure continues next page

Figure 4.1 Snapshot of the Annual School Census Survey (2012–13) in Ghana *(continued)*

ACADEMIC Qualifications	CODE
MSLC	01
BECE	02
GCE O'LEVEL	03
SSCE	04
GCE A'LEVEL	05
DIPLOMA	06
DEGREE	07
POST GRADUATE CERTIFICATE	08
POST GRADUATE DIPLOMA	09
MASTERS DEGREE	10
PHD	11
TECHNICIAN	12
HND	13
NO DATA	99

RANKS	CODE
MSLC/BECE	01
GCE 'O' LEVEL	02
SSCE	03
GCE 'A' LEVEL	04
CLASS TEACHER (Unconfirmed)	05
SNR. SUPERVISOR INSTRUCTOR	06
SUPERVISOR INSTRUCTOR	07
PRIN. TECHNICAL INSTRUCTOR	08
SRN. TECHNICAL INSTRUCTOR	09
SENIOR INSTRUCTOR	10
TECHNICAL INSTRUCTOR GD. I	11
TECHNICAL INSTRUCTOR GD. II	12
SUPT. II	13
SUPT. I	14
SNR. SUPT. II	15
SNR. SUPT. I	16
PRINCIPAL SUPT.	17
ASST. DIRECTOR	18
DIRECTOR II	19
DIRECTOR I	20
ASST. DIRECTOR II	22
DEPUTY DIRECTOR	23
CLASS TEACHER CONFIRMED	24
NO DATA	99

PROFESSIONAL Qualifications	CODE
CERT 'A'	01
DIPLOMA	02
DEGREE	03
POST GRADUATE CERTIFICATE	04
POST GRADUATE DIPLOMA	05
MASTERS DEGREE	06
PHD	07
NO DATA	99

MANAGEMENT Unit	CODE
A.M.E. ZION	01
ANGLICAN	02
ROMAN CATHOLIC	03
EVANGELICAL PRESBYTERIAN	04
GARRISON	05
ISLAMIC	06
L.A/D.A/M.A/BODY CORPORATE	07
METHODIST	08
PRESBYTERIAN	09
SALVATION ARMY	10
SEVENTH DAY ADVENTIST	11
T.I. AHMADIYYA	12
BAPTIST	13
PRIVATE	14
D.A/R.C	15
ASSEMBLIES OF GOD	16
L.A/SALVATION ARMY	17
L.A/ANGLICAN	18
L.A/SDA	19
POLICE	20
L.A/PRESBY	21
L.A/METHODIST	22
L.A/E.P	23
PENTECOST	24
OTHER MANAGEMENT TYPE	25
NO DATA	99

Source: Ministry of Education, Ghana.

Lessons Learned from World Bank Education Management Information System Operations
http://dx.doi.org/10.1596/978-1-4648-1056-5

Maldives: Third Education and Training Project (P055944), 2000–07

The project objective was to improve education quality and efficiency, increase equitable access, strengthen institutional capacity, and develop professional skills in the national labor force. To this end, the project focused on developing an EMIS to collect data on education statistics, with special reference to student enrollment and transition rates, teachers by gender and location, and participation and achievement rates (see table 4.1 for the contents of the Statistical Handbook). The project made an important contribution in the form of setting up a core EMIS over the project period to collect data on student enrollment and transition rates as well as teachers by gender and location. Since 2004 the Ministry of Education (MoE) has been able to publish reliable annual education statistics. Some further modification of the EMIS is needed to facilitate the collection of data on teachers' employment history, teacher development activities, school facilities, higher education, examination results, repetition rates, school

Table 4.1 Table of Contents, *Maldives Handbook on Education Statistics* (2014)

Table of contents	Pages
INTRODUCTION	1
SECTION 1: ENROLMENT TRENDS & ANALYSIS	
Student enrolment 2001 to 2011 by provider	2–3
Transition rate from primary to secondary by atoll	4
Net & gross enrolment rate by gender	5–8
Enrolment trends by level of education	9–15
Enrolment by level, regions & provider	16
Enrolment in Male' and Atolls by grade and Sex	17–21
Enrolment pre-primary age in grade by provider	22
Enrolment primary age in grade (All Schools)	23
Enrolment secondary age in grade (All Schools)	24
New entrants to grade 1	25
Home Atoll of Students studying in Male' schools	
SECTION 2: SCHOOLS	26
No. of schools and Enrolments of Male' and Atolls	27
Frequency distribution of schools	28
No. of schools (Primary & Secondary)	29
Frequency distribution of pre-schools	30
No. of government schools and their enrolments (Male' and Atolls)	31
No. of community schools and their enrolments (Male' and Atolls)	32
No. of private schools and their enrolments (Male' and Atolls)	33
No. of community & private schools and enrolments (Male' and Atolls)	34
No. of schools (government, community & private) by (Male' and Atolls)	35
Student enrolment in Male' & Atolls by level & institutions	36

table continues next page

Table 4.1   Table of Contents, *Maldives Handbook on Education Statistics* (2014) *(continued)*

Source: Ministry of Education, Maldives.

supervision, and student assessment to enable the system to be better used as a policy-making tool. Given the distances and natural barriers between widely spread-out schools, the further development of the EMIS must address both the development of additional modules for data collection and their linkages to schools.

Lao People's Democratic Republic: A Second Education Development Project (P078113), 2004–14

The objective of the project was (1) increased primary enrollment and completion in the 19 poorest districts in the six poorest provinces, (2) quality improved, and (3) capacities strengthened to develop policies and strategies to monitor and manage primary education. The EMIS component focused on strengthening information systems to support improved collection, analysis, reporting, filing, storing, and maintenance of data and information. The project supported the strengthening of its EMIS system, including the installation of improved software. Although initial delays were seen in setting up the EMIS, the Ministry and international technical assistance were able to overcome these challenges and improve overall data collection and statistics reporting. Some of the main achievements include (1) publishing statistical yearbooks and other education information online and making them accessible via the web or mobile applications, (2) providing education information disaggregated by gender and ethnicity, (3) incorporating personnel and financial information down to school levels, and (4) linking EMIS data collection and analysis with GIS. The EMIS team has also provided extensive training at the central, provincial, district and school levels on a range of information collection, analysis, and management aspects, including the use of GIS.

Sierra Leone: Rehabilitation of Basic Education (P074320), 2003–09

The objective of the project was to assist the government of Sierra Leone (GOSL) to reestablish education services and prepare the grounds for building up the sector. Specifically, the project would (1) assist participating schools to achieve basic operational levels and (2) build up the capacity of Ministry of Education, Youth and Sports (MEYS) to plan and manage the delivery of education services.

The EMIS component focused on financing activities aimed at setting up an EMIS that would include data on schools, staffing, and finances. The proposed EMIS was to have up-to-date school-based, staff-related, and financial data. The project was to finance four Annual School Surveys that would provide an essential part of the information to be integrated in the EMIS system. By project completion the EMIS had been established but was not fully functional. Although the statistical yearbook for first EMIS census was published, annual school surveys were not conducted as planned. As at the time of the implementation completion report (ICR), although plans were in place to recruit a director for the EMIS, no one had been recruited yet, because of a lack of qualified candidates. The most recent data available on enrollment by class at that time were 2003–04, and the most recent data on teachers were 2000–01. Detailed enrollment data have been collected for the 2007–08 academic year, but the Ministry did not have capacity to input the data electronically. The lack of education statistics made monitoring project outcomes and critical education sector indicators impossible, such as primary school completion rate, pupil teacher ratio, and percentage of qualified teachers.

CHAPTER 5

Conclusion: Lessons Learned

In this report we have placed the Education Management Information System (EMIS) challenges into four broad areas with examples from country operations. These challenges have been complemented with a list of possible solutions based on the Systems Approach for Better Education Results (SABER)-EMIS framework, which offer key takeaways for the project teams (table 5.1):

- **Unclear vision and limited buy-in:** Many projects remained unsuccessful because of the lack of shared vision on the functionalities of the EMIS as well as because of limited government support and buy-in. To overcome these challenges, the project teams need to focus on developing a legal framework to support EMIS operations. This would lay the groundwork for the establishment of the EMIS. Moreover, conversations should be made with various education stakeholders across the education system to make them understand the importance of data for decision making. Building a "data-driven" culture in many countries is at least a 20-year process, which should be factored in at the planning stage. Training of top decision makers would also be a useful step at this point to avoid conflicts and bring everyone to a common consensus.

- **Absence of institutionalization:** Regular changes in senior management of the government is a common characteristic in many countries. Changes in leadership result in project delays because of varied interests and priorities. Again, having a written legal mandate would be helpful in pushing for reforms. A clearly defined organization structure with a mission statement, structured workflow, and defined roles and responsibilities would be helpful. A legal policy with a dedicated EMIS budget for its operations would avoid funding issues and dependence on donors for EMIS sustainability. An EMIS should be seen as a technical issue but should be raised to the policy level.

- **Unreliable and poor quality of data:** A common problem related to an EMIS in many countries is the collection of inconsistent, incomplete, and unreliable education data. A starting point to solve this issue is to have a well-defined

Table 5.1 Key Takeaways: Mapping Challenges to Solutions

Solutions	Challenges						
	Leadership		Data			System	Operational
	Unclear vision and limited buy-in	Absence of institutionalization	Unreliable and poor quality of data	Untimely production and dissemination of data	Limited use of data for decision making	Integration issues	Capacity and coordination issues
Legal framework	✓		✓	✓	✓	✓	✓
Organizational structure		✓					✓
Human resources							✓
Infrastructural capacity			✓	✓		✓	✓
Budget	✓	✓					
Data-driven culture	✓				✓		
Data architecture						✓	✓
Data coverage			✓			✓	
Data analytics					✓	✓	
Dynamic system						✓	
Serviceability						✓	
Methodological soundness			✓		✓	✓	
Accuracy and reliability			✓	✓			
Integrity		✓	✓	✓			
Periodicity and timeliness				✓			
Openness to EMIS users				✓			
Operational use					✓		✓
Accessibility				✓			
Effectiveness in disseminating findings				✓			

infrastructure in place that supports data collection, analysis, processing, and dissemination. In addition, discussions should be held with various stakeholders on the type of policy questions they want the data to be able to answer to ensure that data collected are not limited to a small number of indicators such as enrollments and class size. Moreover, sound validation mechanisms (internal and external) must be in place to verify data accuracy and reliability. A code of conduct should be developed for EMIS staff to ensure that the staff exercise professionalism when performing their duties.

- **Untimely production and dissemination of data:** Regular production and dissemination of data are another area of concern. There are often delays in the production and dissemination of a final statistics yearbook to the public. A strategic data dissemination strategy should be in place for publishing data via websites, the annual statistics handbook, and other communication channels. User-friendly platforms should be made available to access data. The dissemination strategy should be bolstered by the policies to support the capacity to disseminate the data.

- **Limited use of data for decision making:** Often because of weak data quality issues, the potential for an EMIS as a tool for making data-driven decisions is not realized. In other cases, even when the EMIS is functioning well, stakeholders do not understand how to use the data. To solve these issues, it is important to create a data-driven culture in the country via workshops and focus group discussions. Charts and graphs should be used to help people understand what the data are trying to reveal. Producing statistics that are easily understandable and accessible would be helpful for using the data.

- **Integration issues:** Technological issues are common in many countries and relate to lack of integration of various information systems, weak Internet access, and availability of computers. Ensuring a sound data architecture with a clearly defined structure of databases, hardware, and software is essential. Moving away from paper-based to IT-based surveys in the form of tablets and phones might simplify the data entry work for schools and ease the process of management and transfer to subnational and national levels.

- **Capacity and coordination issues:** Operational issues revolve around inadequate funding, procurement issues, and lack of coordination between various donors and government as well as weak capacity issues. To overcome these problems, it is important to ensure that the institutionalized processes are sound with clearly outlined mission and duties. Investments should be channeled toward improving the local capacity of the EMIS staff so that dependence on outside support is reduced. A dedicated budget should be allocated toward EMIS operations so that the system continues to work even after the project comes to an end.

Lessons Learned from World Bank Education Management Information System Operations
http://dx.doi.org/10.1596/978-1-4648-1056-5

Based on the findings from the operational experiences and analytical work, the problems in the EMIS value chain are categorized into five stages (figure 5.1).

The frequencies of the occurrence of these problems were mapped to each of these five stages to find that the operational phase faced the maximum number of issues relating to leadership, coordination, and capacity development (figure 5.2).

- **Pre-start:** This is the stage when an EMIS has not been developed in a country as a means to collect data on education statistics. Common issues at this stage revolve around the difficulty in understanding the functions and uses of an EMIS. A systemic diagnostic of an EMIS from policy intent to implementation would prove helpful. Regular conversations should be held among various education stakeholders to understand their aspirations, identify policy questions that they want the data to be able to answer, and then link those policy questions with the education indicators to be captured by EMIS.

- **Input:** This is the stage when the necessary investment into an EMIS starts to take place. Common issues that arise during this stage include limited availability of funds to support a system, technology (hardware, software) supporting the system, and training of staff to use the system. At this stage, it is important to clearly align the EMIS goals with the allocated project budget

Figure 5.1 Problems in EMIS Value Chain

Figure 5.2 Number of Challenges at Each Stage of the Project Cycle

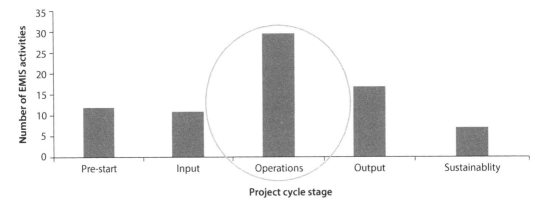

and government needs, including maintenance costs. Procurement of any software and hardware should be made after consultations with the relevant stakeholders, especially schools, to identify their needs and assess the possibility of integration of different databases into the EMIS.

- **Operations:** Most issues arise during the operational phase when the project is rolled out. These issues range from the procurement of infrastructure for the EMIS to the lack of coordination between the different units in the Ministry and project teams, as well as continuous changes in the leadership. This mainly occurs because of a time lag between the launch of the project and implementation of the system, as well as changes in the EMIS objectives.

- **Output:** This is the stage when an EMIS has been developed in a country. Problems that occur in this stage relate to the quality of the data collected, processed, and disseminated. Considerable issues exist with the reliability and accuracy of the data collected from schools, as well as limited utilization of the collected data by education stakeholders. Creating mechanisms for building capacity at all levels of education system, validating the quality of data collected, creating awareness on the importance of data, as well as providing open access to the data result in increased transparency, accountability, and improved quality.

- **Sustainability:** The most common problem across all countries is the inability to sustain the system once it has been established. This is mainly because of a lack of continued investment into the EMIS, linking the EMIS to M&E components of the project, as well as a weak data-driven culture in the society. Continuous investment is needed into research and development activities such as publication of reports using data generated from the EMIS. World Bank support should be reduced in a phased manner that helps develop local capacity.

To fully understand and inform the design and development of an EMIS, it is critical to examine both the policies and programs as well as implementation of the EMIS at the different levels of the education system (central government, local government, and schools). In so doing, the project team is able to gauge the alignment of policies and programs with utilization and to ultimately provide suggestions that bolster the efficiency, sustainability, and accountability relationships of the EMIS.

Based on the different problem areas discussed above, a quick and flexible EMIS checklist has been designed to support the teams during the project. This checklist includes a list of items to guide the teams at each stage of EMIS development (table 5.2). This checklist can be conducted simply as checklist, with the teams working their way down the list, or it can be used as a series of questions to guide a focus group. Either way, it is recommended that the investigator ensure that all of the questions are answered, unless information does not exist to answer the question.

Lessons Learned from World Bank Education Management Information System Operations
http://dx.doi.org/10.1596/978-1-4648-1056-5

Table 5.2 EMIS Checklist

Project preparation

☐ Policies/Legal Framework:

  ☐ Written law mandating data-driven decision making

☐ Scope/Plan:

  ☐ Assessment of existing EMIS

  ☐ Staged plan for EMIS implementation

☐ Alignment:

  ☐ EMIS goals aligned with education goals and other government initiatives

  ☐ Identify existing databases, plan for integration within the education system and with external agencies

☐ Sustainability:

  ☐ Long-term vision and commitment to project from the government

  ☐ Develop relationships and common direction with stakeholders

☐ Budget:

  ☐ Realistic budget allocated for EMIS

  ☐ Alignment of EMIS goals with budget

  ☐ Thoughtful breakdown of EMIS budget (capacity building, professional development, staff, infrastructure)

Operational phase

☐ Strong start of the project by reducing the time gap between launch of the project and its implementation

☐ Ensure minimum changes in EMIS goals during EMIS implementation

☐ Appoint nodal officer responsible for collection and dissemination of data (at central and regional government levels)

☐ Reduce delays in data collection process

☐ Utilization of data for decision making (from the beginning ensure access of information to all stakeholders and effective utilization of data)

☐ Ensure regular/meaningful capacity-building activities

☐ Integration of databases

Ending the project

☐ Reduce World Bank support in a phased manner

☐ Continue to provide necessary support to countries (e.g., capacity building, regional initiatives)

☐ Ensure long-term sustainability and continuity of operations:

  ☐ Regular audits

  ☐ Upgrading of technology/systems

  ☐ Ensure efficiencies

CHAPTER 6

Examples of EMIS Implementation beyond World Bank Support

EMIS in the Philippines

The Basic Education Information System (BEIS) serves as the primary management information system of the Department of Education, helping education planners make important policy decisions on improving the quality of education system in the Philippines. In particular, it collects statistical information on basic education inputs such as enrollments, pupil-teacher ratios, and school infrastructure.

Besides BEIS, other information systems reside within the Department of Education: (a) the Human Resources Information System (HRIS), which collects information on people (teachers and administrative staff) employed in the system; (b) the Material Resources Information System (MRIS), which contains information on school facilities such as classrooms, desks, and other logistic components; and (c) the Financial Resources Information System (FRIS), which includes information on all the finances needed for the development of the system (figure 6.1). All four systems work in coordination with each other, but they are not integrated. In addition, an Education Management Information System (EMIS) toolbox interface helps in converting the data produced by EMIS into useful analytics and preparing Basic Education Report Cards annually.

EMIS in Cambodia

The government of Cambodia places special emphasis on EMIS as a tool to inform education planning, monitoring, evaluating, and budgeting and for other activities that are essential for monitoring the progress of the education performance. To this end, the government recently developed an EMIS Master Plan (2014–18)[1] that provides detailed information on the strategic plan for the EMIS over the next five years.

Figure 6.1 Snapshot of the Data Generated by EMIS, the Philippines

Pupil:Seatratio	Color code		Remarks
Less than 0.49		Blue	Two-seats per pupil even in one-shift schools
0.50 –0.69		Sky Blue	Surplus seat provision
0.70 –0.89		Green	Generous seat provision
0.90 –1.00		Yellow	Adequate in one-shift schools
1.01 –1.99		Gold	Adequate in two-shift schools
2.00 –2.99		Orange	More than 2 pupils per seat; Inadequate in two-shift schools
More than 3.00		Red	More than 3 pupils per seat ; Severe shortage in two-shift schools
No Seats Available		Black	No existing seats

DepEd District Data Bulletin

School Year : 2002-2003

Region : 08 Region VIII - Eastern Visayas
Division : 001 Biliran
District : 001 Almeria

SCHOOL ID	SCHOOL NAME	SCHOOL DISTRICT NAME	Legislative District	Total Enrolment	Total Instructional Rooms	Pupil : Classroom Ratio	Color Code
104528	Sallan PS	Abucay	1	72	6	12.00	Blue
104542	Bankawang ES	Bagac	2	274	6	45.67	Blue
104500	Sta. Isabel PS	Dinalupihan	1	138	3	46.00	Yellow
104549	Townsite PS	Marveles	2	50	1	50.00	Yellow
104524	Bacong ES	Limay	2	1,002	20	50.10	Yellow
104570	Bangal ES	Dinalupihan	1	518	10	51.80	Gold
104577	J.C. Payumo Jr. Mem. ES	Dinalupihan	1	489	9	54.33	Gold
104563	Orani North ES	Orani	1	2,441	36	67.81	Red
104543	Ipag ES	Marveles	2	818	12	68.17	Red
104569	Pulo ES	Orani	1	139	2	69.50	Red
104530	Evia Aeta School	Orion	2	24	0		Black

Source: Lilia and Deogracias 2004.

The EMIS resides under the Planning Department of the Ministry of Education, Youth and Sport (MoEYS) in Cambodia (see figure 6.2 for the EMIS Cycle). An annual census form is used to collect data from schools, which is then sent to the district and provincial offices, before it reaches the central government. A separate three-or-four-page form exists for each level of the education system, pre-primary, primary, and secondary as well as district and municipal education services on the following attributes: teachers and students, income, some facilities, staff of provinces, cities, and districts (figure 6.3). The EMIS Centre is the focal point for collection and dissemination of education statistics. All schools are required to complete four copies: one to be kept in school for reference purposes, one each to be sent to DEO and PES, and the last copy to be sent to the EMIS Centre at the central level in the Department of Planning for checking, editing, data entry, and analysis (EMIS Master Plan 2014–18). Once the data have been collected, the MoEYS has a comprehensive dissemination strategy where the produced statistics are distributed to the following stakeholders: (a) National Senate, (b) National Assembly, (c) Cabinet of the Prime Minister, (d) Authority of Council Minister, (e) embassies in the Kingdom of Cambodia, (f) national and international organizations (UNESCO, UNICEF,

Figure 6.2 EMIS Cycle in Cambodia

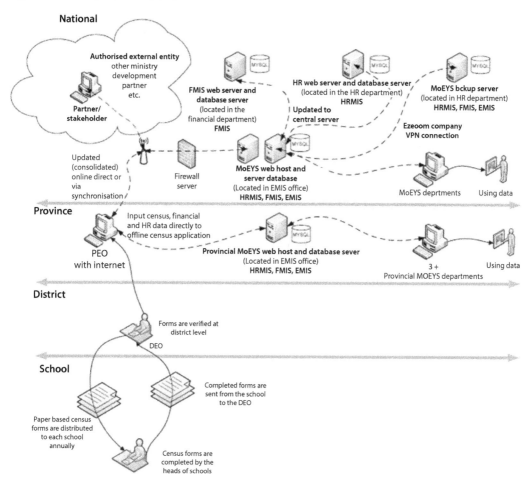

Source: EMIS Master Plan (2014–18), MoEYS.

UNDP, ADB, other NGOs), (g) ministries relevant to education, (h) departments of the Ministry of Education Youth and Sport, (i) Provincial Education Services (PES) and District of Education offices (DEO), and (j) public schools (EMIS office, Department of Planning, MoEYS).

EMIS in the Republic of Korea

The National Education Information System (NEIS) is a web-based integrated administration system, housed within the Ministry of Education and Human Resource Department, which is responsible for collecting education data from

Figure 6.3 Snapshot of the School Census Form

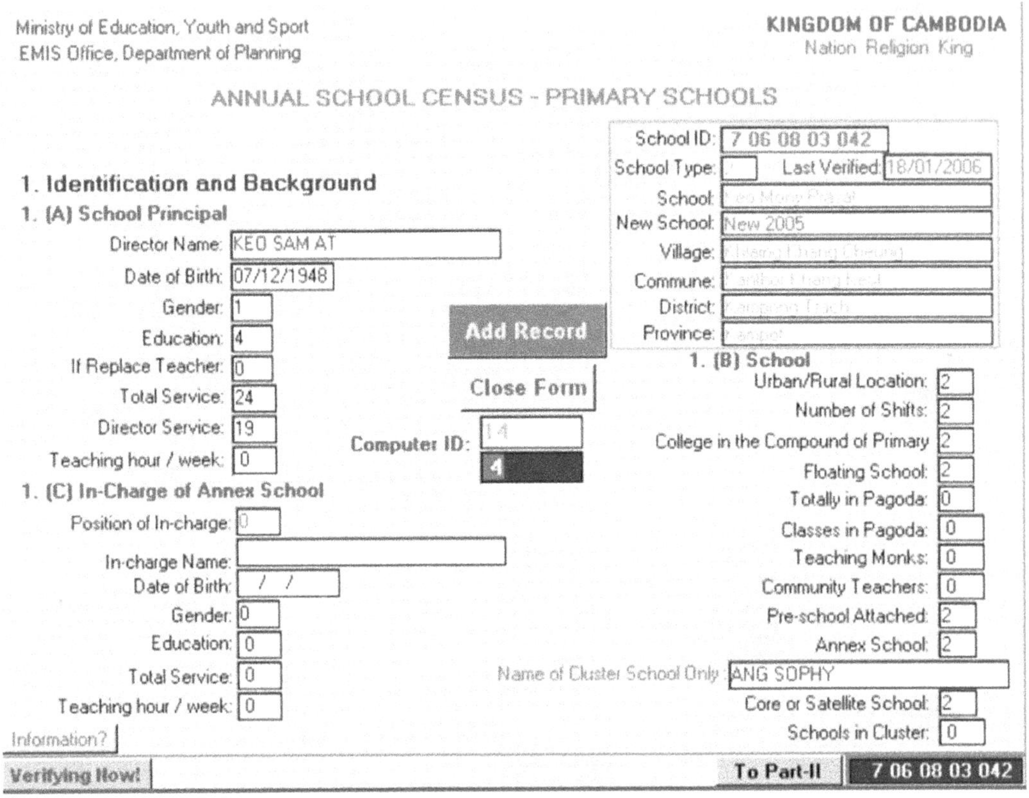

Ministry of Education, Youth and Sport
EMIS Office, Department of Planning

KINGDOM OF CAMBODIA
Nation Religion King

ANNUAL SCHOOL CENSUS - PRIMARY SCHOOLS

School ID: 7 06 08 03 042
School Type: ☐   Last Verified: 18/01/2006

1. Identification and Background
1. (A) School Principal
Director Name: KEO SAM AT
Date of Birth: 07/12/1948
Gender: 1
Education: 4
If Replace Teacher: 0
Total Service: 24
Director Service: 19
Teaching hour / week: 0
1. (C) In-Charge of Annex School
Position of In-charge: 0
In-charge Name:
Date of Birth: / /
Gender: 0
Education: 0
Total Service: 0
Teaching hour / week: 0
Information?

School: Keo Mong Phai 3
New School: New 2005
Village:
Commune:
District:
Province:

Add Record

Close Form

Computer ID: 14
4

1. (B) School
Urban/Rural Location: 2
Number of Shifts: 2
College in the Compound of Primary: 2
Floating School: 2
Totally in Pagoda: 0
Classes in Pagoda: 0
Teaching Monks: 0
Community Teachers: 0
Pre-school Attached: 2
Annex School: 2

Name of Cluster School Only ANG SOPHY
Core or Satellite School: 2
Schools in Cluster: 0

Verifying Now!   To Part-II 7 06 08 03 042

Source: UNESCO 2008.

primary and secondary schools, local education offices, and other education institutions to monitor and manage education performance (figure 6.4). The NEIS was developed to serve the following purposes:

- Improving efficiency, transparency, and convenience in education administration (standard and system-based work process)
- Reducing teachers' work load and raising the quality of education by reorganizing the work process
- Providing high-quality educational services to citizens:
  - One-stop online issuance of official certificates
  - Online service for parents (providing information on children's school activities through NEIS)

It contains information on a wide variety of education statistics such as students' grades, their activity in school and performance, and human resources data (payroll, facilities for staff and nonstaff). This information is readily available for

Figure 6.4 Republic of Korea National Education Information System

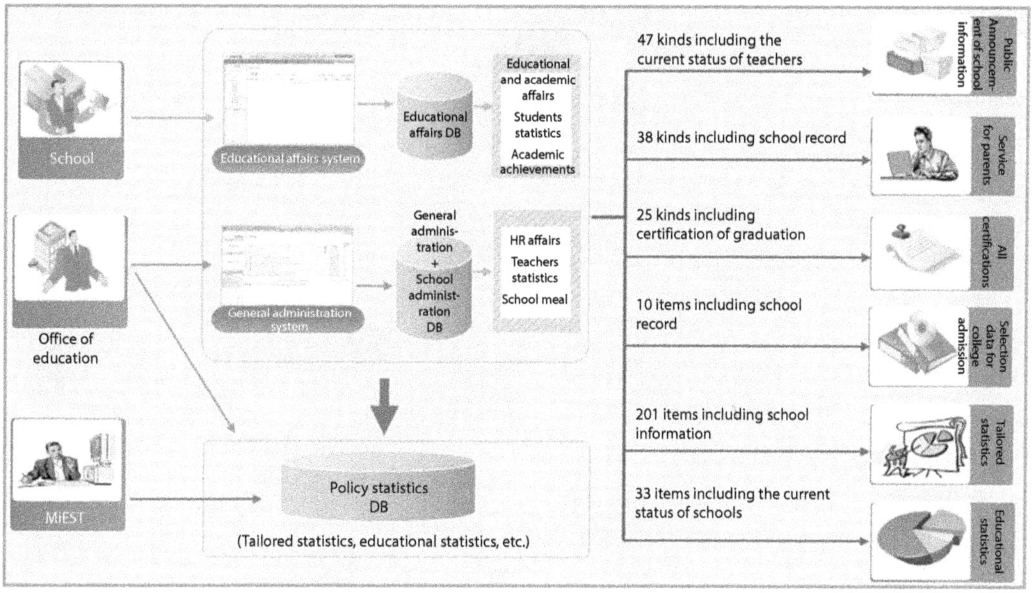

Source: Republic of Korea Education Research and Information Service.

access to parents and students online. This system guarantees the students' and parents' right to know and, consequently, increases parent and local community interest and participation. It is also useful if students need to switch schools for any reason; their information is stored in an online database that follows them to whichever school they attend (Severin 2011).

Note

1. EMIS Master Plan.

CHAPTER 7

Other World Bank Activities Relevant to EMIS

In the field of building information systems, it is important to coordinate among sectors. Working in silos consists of negative consequences, misalignments, and sustainability issues that have led to failures, missed opportunities, and increased expenditures because funding these systems tend to be expensive. Breaking silos and helping stakeholders to see their contributions to particular goals in an integrated manner is important toward achieving the Sustainable Development Goals.

A major issue across all education systems around the world is the need for a national identity. Linking of the identity with the education system is crucial to monitor and track performance of students, teachers, and management of schools. The potential impact of these identity systems can have far-reaching implications on service delivery and management of education information systems. Leveraging these systems to track students and teachers and electronically validate academic and employment histories can certainly contribute to the growth of the education systems while providing the necessary data for government to make interventions.

Need for ID4D Systems

Across different global practices such as health, social protection, and finance and markets, projects have activities related to information systems. Only recently has the ID4D—Identification for Development—initiative (launched in 2015) materialized as the first step toward harmonizing various cross-practice projects. The ID4D initiative aims to bring different units of the World Bank under one umbrella to achieve the objective of providing a unique legal identity and enable digital ID-based services to all. Providing a legal identity for all (including birth registration) by 2030 is a target shared by the international community as part of the Sustainable Development Goals. Moreover, there has been an increasing demand for these services across countries (figure 7.1).

Figure 7.1 Civil Registration and Identification Trends in 198 Economies (1960–2014)

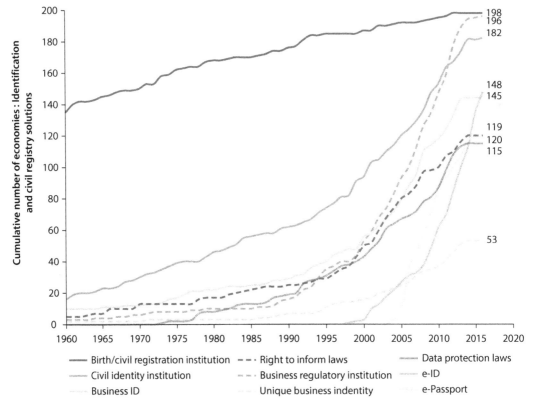

Source: World Bank 2015b.
Note: ID = Identity.

Benefits

In relation to students, the ID system can be put to use to track students in the following ways: (a) simplifying procedures to seek school admission, (b) establishing mechanisms to verify entitlements such as scholarships and grants, (c) tracking attendance, drop-out rates, transitions, and transfers to different schools, (d) tracking the education history of a student over his or her life, (e) monitoring employment status after school completion, (f) preventing misuse of data by identifying ghost student and teachers, and most importantly (g) monitoring student learning and designing interventions aimed at improving the academic performance of weak students.

In the case of teachers, ID systems can be used to track data about teacher demographics such as age, gender, academic, and professional qualifications, as well as their salaries and payroll transactions. The system could also be used monitor teacher training activities and completion of professional development courses. The ID system can also be useful to track information about schools such as (a) management of financial and material resources, (b) asset allocation, (c) civil works, and (d) recruitment of staff.

Portfolio of ID4D Projects

Over the last 30 years, the World Bank Group has financed 142 projects related to developing a unique national identity to provide digital ID-based services to all due to the growing demand for these systems across countries. The maximum concentration of these investments are in Africa (47), followed by LAC (29) and ECA (21) (figure 7.2). Out of these, 63 (44 percent) are currently active, 56 (40 percent) are closed, and 23 (16 percent) are in the pipeline (figure 7.3).

Figure 7.4 shows the distribution of these projects by the Global Practice. Maximum projects (82) are concentrated in the Governance Global Practice, followed by Social Protection (31), mainly because the development of ID systems in most developing countries is tied to governance and administration and provision of social protection schemes such as cash transfers.

The focus of the projects was mainly on creating the following registries: (a) national ID and civil registries for birth registration and creating of national identity, (b) beneficiary registry to determine the recipients of social protection schemes, (c) taxpayer registry to determine the number of taxpayers, (d) business registry to account for the number of businesses, (e) civil service registry to determine the number of government officials and account for the wages received, and (d) other miscellaneous registries. Each project could be designed to create more than one registry (figure 7.5). Maximum projects undertaken were designed to develop identities to enable effective delivery of public services,

Figure 7.2 Number of ID4D Projects, by Region
percent

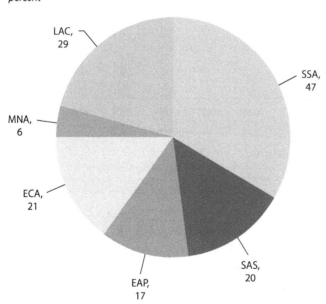

Source: ID4D database 2015.
Note: EAP = East Asia and Pacific, ECA = Europe and Central Asia, LAC = Latin America and Caribbean, MNA = Middle East and North Africa, SAS = South Asia, SSA = Sub-Saharan Africa.

Figure 7.3 Number of Active Projects

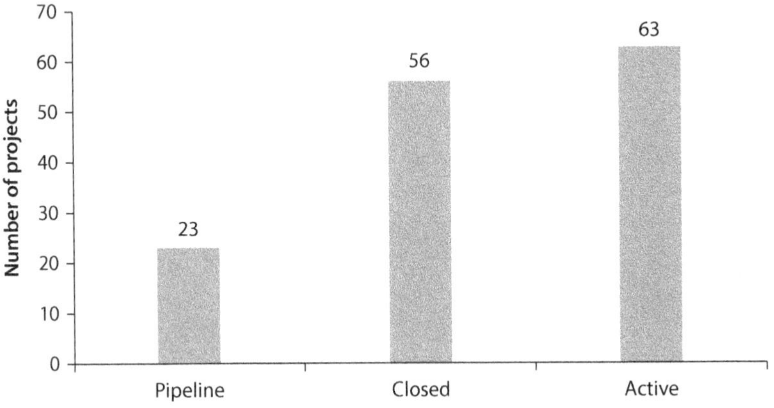

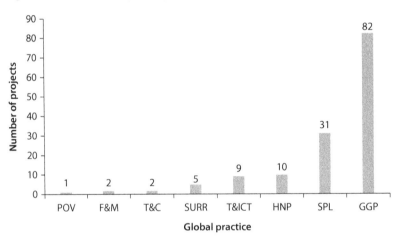

Source: ID4D database 2015.

Figure 7.4 Number of Projects, by Global Practice

Source: ID4D Database 2015.
Note: POV = Poverty; F&M = Finance & Markets; T&C = Trade & Competitiveness; SURR = Social, Urban & Rural Development; T&ICT = Transport & Information and Communication Technology; HNP = Health, Nutrition, and Population; SPL = Social Protection and Labor; GGP = Governance Global Practice.

reflecting the importance of the ID systems to improve the governance and management of education, health, and social protection programs.

The structure and technology of identity systems differ across countries. For example, Estonia uses a sophisticated civil registration system using a digital system issuing a chip-based identity card with a photograph. This mechanism works well in a developed country with a good education system, where people are familiar with online services and a civil registry is developed. In contrast, India uses a biometric system using fingerprints and iris scans to issue a unique 12-digit

Figure 7.5 Projects Related to Registration Systems

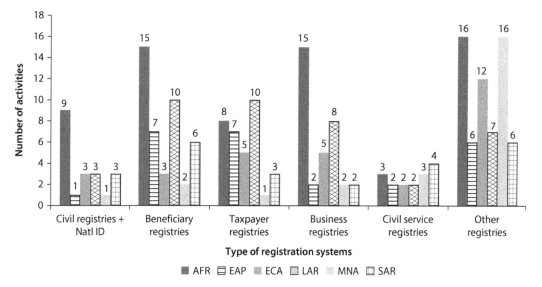

Source: ID4D Database 2015.

number (Atick et al. 2014b). Similarly, Ghana and Pakistan also use biometrics to issue the identity cards (table 7.1).

Various examples have been selected to illustrate the importance of identity systems in ensuring effective delivery of social protection schemes and health care services.

- In **Thailand**, the national civil registration database is established and maintained by the National Civil Registration Office, Ministry of Interior (MOI). By law, this office is responsible for registering all births, deaths, marriages, divorces, and migrations. A unique 13-digit identification number is generated for each Thai citizen at the time that their birth is registered in the national civil registration database. National ID cards are issued to citizens when they reach the age of seven years old. This national identification number is used by health care providers to verify eligibility, track delivered services, settle claims, and build a shared medical record for each patient. The use of the national ID numbers has led to improvements in the efficiency and transparency of the national social health protection system's management as well as prevented misuse of public resources (ILO 2015).

- In **Costa Rica**, universal health coverage is provided to all poor, who are identified using the National Identity Card Number. When an individual seeks services in a health center, these centers can identify individuals according to socioeconomic status through a household survey with 267 variables including health and risk factors that the health service team administers. The health center will confirm the information and visit and interview the household

Table 7.1 Common Models of ID Systems

Estonia	*India*
Governing body: Citizen and Migration Board, Ministry of Internal Affairs	**Governing body:** Unique Identification Authority of India (UIDAI), under Planning Commission of India
Registration type: Civil registration	**Registration type:** Biometrics (10 fingerprints and iris)
Credential: Identity card with a photograph and chip for security purposes	**Credential:** 12-digit unique ID number called "Aadhaar" (no physical credential)
Target population: 1.3 million people	**Target population:** 1.2 billion people
Use of ID: Personal ID number	**Use of ID:** Aadhaar number, along with demographic, biometric, or password

Ghana	*Pakistan*
Governing body: National Identity Authority, within the Office of the President	**Governing body:** National Database and Registration Authority (autonomous body)
Registration type: Biometrics (fingerprints)	**Registration type:** Biometrics (fingerprints)
Credential: National Identity Card ("Ghana Card") and smartcard	**Credential:** National Identity Card with a photograph, smartcard, and mobile ID
Target population: 25 million people	**Target population:** 180 million people
Use of ID: National Identity Card and biometrics	**Use of ID:** Smartcards, mobile phones, and biometrics

Source: Atick et al. 2014b.

before formally enrolling the individual. The identification of the individual is based on the national identity card number and a CCSS (Social Security of Costa Rica) beneficiary card, which contains this and other information relevant for administrative purposes (type of beneficiary, employer, work address, and so forth). Individuals enrolled do not need to be recertified and remain as beneficiaries of the noncontributory regime unless their work status changes and they enroll in the contributory regime (Montenegro Torres 2013).

- In **India**, digital IDs enable targeted cash transfers to a bank account number that is linked to a unique identifier. This ensures that those who are entitled to receive subsidies or benefits are actually getting them. For example, in India's fuel subsidy program, by implementing cash transfers to Aadhaar-linked bank accounts for the purchase of liquefied petroleum gas cylinders, realizable savings are about 11–14 percent, or $1 billion per year when applied throughout the country. This is just one of many subsidy programs in India that are being converted to direct transfers using a digital ID, impacting more than $11 billion per year (World Bank 2015d).

- **Pakistan's** National ID (NADRA) to implement the Benazir Income Support Program (BISP) has been a role model for many South Asian countries such as Bangladesh and Nepal. Established in 2000, Pakistan's national ID agency, NADRA, is one of the earliest developing country ID agencies to use biometrics to ensure unique ID numbers for its citizens. With estimated coverage of the adult population at almost 90 percent, the National ID Card has become the dominant form of identification for most transactions. Most recently, NADRA has worked closely with the BISP to ensure robust identification of the beneficiaries of the country's largest cash transfer program and has helped implement an e-payments system linked to this robust form of identification (World Bank 2015c).

- In **Peru**, legislation passed in 1995 created a consolidated, sole-purpose agency called National Registry of Identification and Civil Status (RENIEC) that is responsible for both civil registry and national IDs. An ID number is generated for adults, and uniqueness is ensured using biometrics. The ID number is now used for the vast majority of public and private transactions—from voting to opening bank accounts—and is used for social programs such as cash transfers and social insurance. In the last decade, huge efforts have been made to identify children through RENIEC; these efforts have important implications for the delivery of certain social programs, such as World Bank–supported nutrition programs for young children. Coverage is almost universal for the adult population and has reached 95 percent for children (World Bank 2015c).

- In 2006, **the Arab Republic of Egypt** implemented a smartcard system for its subsidized food program that now covers three-fourths of its population. The Ministry of State for Administrative Development (MSAD) maintains the registry of the individual members of families that have a "family card," which entitles them to receive subsidized food under a program run by another ministry. The same card is used for social assistance payments from a third ministry. The transaction information flows to the MSAD and is then accessible to the other two ministries, which use the information to allocate cash and food, respectively, and to track their transactions. Although there are different points of transaction—food shops and post offices for cash—the transaction process and the back-end information system are the same (World Bank 2015c).

The examples illustrate the importance of identity systems to the bottom 40 percent of the population to have better access to job opportunities, services, and finance. A robust identity system involves capturing the unique identity of each individual in a national identity registry. The national registry can then be used across sectors—from education and health care to transportation and urban development—for the delivery of services, both public and private (figure 7.6).

Figure 7.6 Potential of Identification Systems to Improve Service Delivery

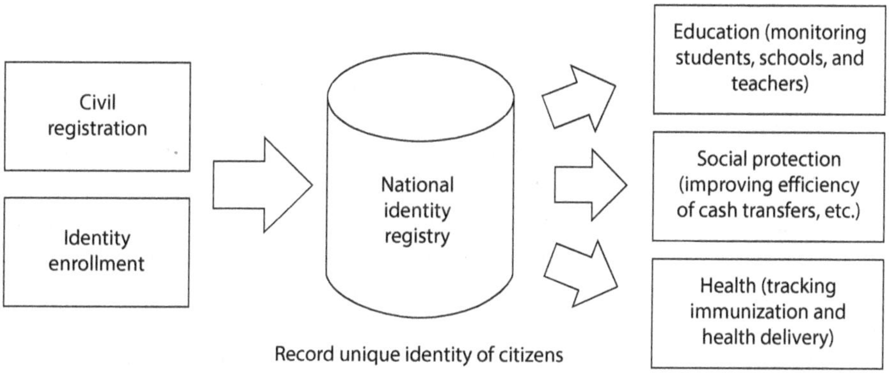

Source: World Bank 2015.

Lessons Learned from World Bank Education Management Information System Operations
http://dx.doi.org/10.1596/978-1-4648-1056-5

Management Information Systems for Social Service Schemes for the Poor

In the case of Social Protection, Management Information Systems (MISs) serve to support social services and to provide information to institutions on the delivery of services. This information enables stakeholders to make adjustments in their planning and allocation decisions, especially for the Cash Transfer Schemes. MISs can have several advantages and can be used in the following forms: (a) a single beneficiary registry, (b) an integrated information system for all social protection programs and for beneficiaries, and (c) a single entry point for beneficiaries to access social protection programs (Bassett, Blanco, and Villalobos 2010).

The following section describes some of the projects undertaken by the World Bank in the area of MIS that were instrumental in monitoring the effective delivery of these services.

Timor-Leste Social Protection Administration Project (P125784), 2011–14

In Timor-Leste, the World Bank entered into a project agreement with the government to improve the management of cash transfer programs in an efficient, reliable, and transparent manner through standardizing information management and strengthening program implementation and management capacity. The entire project was dedicated toward the improvement of the information systems. As such, it had two objectives: (a) to support MIS development and service delivery innovation and (b) to support capacity-building activities. Through the project, the Ministry of Social Solidarity (MSS) has developed a MIS that will improve the implementation of the social programs by integrating the databases of three existing cash transfer programs: (a) Bolsa da Mae, (b) the Elderly and Disabled program, and (c) the National Disasters Program. The new system is intended to allow for cross-checks and updates, monitoring transactions, facilitating payments, allowing grievance management, and generating reports on program implementation. In addition, the project places special emphasis on developing skills, capability, and expertise to ensure that staff at the Ministry are able to maintain, update, and modify the database as required.

Promoting an Inclusive, Equitable, and Efficient Social Protection System in Colombia (P106708), 2009–10

In Colombia a social protection project was initiated to strengthen the system in the country. To increase the efficiency of the system, the operation sought improved information systems, rationalization, and simplification in several programs, such as public pensions, extreme poverty alleviation, or training. These policy actions built upon previous achievements in the different areas supported by the operation, such as the implementation of a unified payment mechanism for social security contributions (PILA: Integrated Contributions Payment System, *Planilla Integrada de Liquidación de Aportes*), the existence of a single registry of participants in social programs (RUAF: Unified Registry of Affiliates, *Registro Unificado de Afiliados*), utilization of a targeting mechanism (SISBEN: System for the Selection of Programs' Beneficiaries, *Sistema de Identificación de Potenciales Beneficiaries de Programas*), and existing regulations and policies to improve income generation opportunities for the poor, among others. In many cases, the operation sought to increase the coverage of these instruments (e.g., PILA, RUAF) to improve their effectiveness (e.g., SISBEN) or to implement improvements and previously designed reforms (e.g., consolidation of public pensions, labor market observatories). The new system allowed programs to more efficiently target their beneficiaries and monitor their activities. It can also play a key role in identifying potential overlaps or synergies between programs.

Bihar (India) Integrated Social Protection Strengthening Project (P118826), 2013–20

In India the World Bank entered into an agreement with the government to strengthen institutional capacity of the Department of Social Welfare and the Rural Development Department to deliver social protection programs and services and expand outreach of social care services for poor and vulnerable households, persons with disabilities, older persons, and widows in the state of Bihar. To this end, one of the objectives of this project was to support the design and implementation of a comprehensive MIS, including (a) setting up an electronic registry of persons with disabilities and older persons, (b) developing a beneficiary database of persons who are currently receiving social pensions, and (c) design and development of transactions-enabled applications for social pensions and social care services. It is expected that investment into MIS would strengthen governance and decision making by providing accurate and timely information to decision makers on the implementation and effectiveness of the programs.

Kenya Cash Transfer for Orphans and Vulnerable Children (CT-OVC) (P111545), 2009–16

The proposed project intended to contribute to strengthening the government's capacity to develop social protection policy, coordinate social protection interventions, and manage the CT-OVC Program at national, provincial, district, and local levels. It would also improve governance and accountability through the implementation of awareness campaigns, a communication strategy, and enhanced oversight and accountability mechanisms (including spot checks and citizens' score cards). It would also improve information and financial management as well as monitoring and evaluation. To this end, the MIS was developed to provide the basic architecture for conditional cash transfers and would be used for identifying and selecting the target population. Although the MIS was built at the national level, plans are now being made for decentralization of the system to the district level.

Lessons Learned from World Bank Education Management Information System Operations
http://dx.doi.org/10.1596/978-1-4648-1056-5

Azerbaijan Social Protection Development Project (P105116), 2008–15

The objective was to improve delivery of labor market and social protection interventions through strengthened institutions, enhanced institutional and human resources capacity, and improved targeting of social safety net programs. To achieve this objective, the project focused on developing a labor market information system to inform policy making. Through the information system, improved targeting through evidence-based decision making can be made possible, and real-time information sharing among various stakeholders will result in fewer errors of inclusion and exclusion and thus more efficient use of public resources. The project activities in the labor market such as increased registration of unemployed and their placement in jobs, enforcement of occupational safety, and modernization of occupational and training standards all would contribute to an overall productivity increase from improvements in the quality of the labor force and more efficient allocation of labor and government revenues from taxes.

These examples highlight the importance of an MIS beyond monitoring and evaluation of projects, as a tool instrumental for effective delivery and management of social services.

Management Information Systems to Improve the Quality of Health Care

Similar to EMIS and SPMIS, the health management information system (HMIS) is sometimes equated with monitoring and evaluation, but this is too reductionist a perspective. In addition to being essential for monitoring and evaluation, the HMIS also serves acts as a red flag system, supporting patient and health facility management, enabling planning, supporting research, permitting health analysis, and enabling communication of health challenges to diverse users. Information is of little value if it is not available in formats that meet the needs of multiple users such as policy makers, planners, managers, health care providers, communities, and individuals. Therefore, dissemination and communication are essential attributes of the health information system (HIS) (WHO 2008).

Below we describe some of the projects undertaken by the World Bank in the HMIS area to improve project management and delivery.

Albania Health System Improvement Project (P144688), 2015–21

In **Albania**, the World Bank and the government are working toward improving the efficiency of care in selected hospitals in the country, through improving the management of information in the health system, and increasing financial access to health services. This includes various complementary and interrelated subcomponents that will move HMIS forward on several critical fronts. (a) The component addresses the need for improved provider-based systems, focusing on the country's regional hospital sector, which significantly impacts the orchestration of services across the spectrum of care. It places emphasis on strengthening referrals to and from both the primary care and tertiary care levels. (b) It also addresses the need to provide the hospitals with a means of adopting the new provider payment methods. (c) In addition, it addresses the need for improved automation in the country's health insurance payer, the HIF, where an improved health insurance information system will be placed. (d) Finally, it provides the foundational activities to support these developments and an institutional home to support and sustain them in the long run.

Swaziland Health, HIV/AIDS, and TB Project (P110156), 2011–16

In **Swaziland**, a MIS was developed to form the basis for a national registry of OVC to establish a beneficiary enrollment, registration, and verification system and setting up a payment delivery mechanism. The MIS is intended to not only facilitate maintaining accurate OVC data, but also to ensure coordination with other ongoing OVC support interventions and monitor the implementation of OVC cash transfers. Human and institutional capacity of the Ministry and government staff will be enhanced at the central and regional levels to ensure effective implementation of the proposed OVC cash transfer pilot and to improve coordination with other ministries, development partners, and NGOs for more comprehensive and efficient OVC support.

Sri Lanka Health Sector Development Project (P050740), 2004–10

In **Sri Lanka**, an MIS was set up to strengthen the stewardship functions of the central Ministry of Health (MOH), including development and effective use of evidence and information systems for policy, planning, monitoring, and management. The motivation was that significant amounts of data get generated through the HMIS without any use of information for planning, and management is limited. The project aim of reducing the delay in compiling the Annual Health Bulletins from four years to under six months from the end of the fiscal year was partly met (under two years). The project supported community surveillance activities for prevention and control of selected communicable diseases. The Family Health Bureau operates an effective system for monitoring the Maternal and Child Health program, but its success in operating its parallel information system has become a hindrance to the government's efforts to harmonize and consolidate the HMIS.

China Basic Health Services Project (P003566), 1998–2007

The project focuses on achieving sustainable health improvement for the populations of poor rural counties through (a) improved allocation and management of health resources, (b) upgraded health facilities at the township level, (c) improved quality and effectiveness of health services and programs, and (d) increased risk sharing and affordability of essential health care for poor families. One of the project activities aimed at improving the collection and use of information for planning and monitoring health programs and the project through (a) improvements to the reporting system and (b) surveys. Funds supported equipment, software development, training, surveys, supervision, and technical support. The establishment of an upgraded information system, supported by specific surveys, improved the information base for decision making. Significant

Lessons Learned from World Bank Education Management Information System Operations
http://dx.doi.org/10.1596/978-1-4648-1056-5

capacity was developed to (a) design, build, and equip improved hospitals, (b) plan technical content and implement public health programs, (c) establish improved referral systems and treatment protocols, (d) manage hospitals more effectively, (d) develop complex administrative processes and the staff capacity to implement schemes, and (e) undertake and sustain reforms.

Turkey Health System Strengthening and Support Project (P152799), 2009–15

The project was set up with the objective of assisting the government in (a) expanding the capacity of the MOH and the Social Security Institution to formulate and effectively implement health policies, health sector regulatory mechanisms, and health insurance functions and (b) supporting the implementation of critical health services delivery reforms (family medicine and hospital autonomy) with the objective of improving access, efficiency, quality, and fiscal sustainability of the health sector. To this end, the project focused on improving the existing HMISs in the country. This involved financing technical assistance, training, and goods in support of the expansion of the MOH National Health Information System. The objective of the HIS was to improve health informatics standards, ensure the confidentiality, security, and privacy principles of personal and institutional health records, establish a data warehouse within the scope of a decision support system, and initiate data mining practices to establish tele-medicine and tele-health systems.

Database of EMIS Projects

Table A.1 Database of EMIS Projects

Project ID	Project	EMIS components	Region	Task team leader	Approval year	Closing year	Project cost (US$, millions)
P132768	Brazil: Pernambuco Equity and Inclusive Growth Development Policy Loan	Subcomponent 1.1: Regional economic development (under Component 1: New Economy—Opportunities for All Pernambucans)	LAC	Joana C. G. Silva	2013	2015	550
P126452	Brazil: Rio Grande Do Norte Regional Development and Governance Project	Subcomponent A3: Improve the quality of basic education and support regional development (under Component A: Integrated Economic and Human Development)	LAC	Maria de Fatima de Sousa Amazonas	2013	2019	400
P129652	Brazil: Sergipe Development through Inclusion Project	2.b.1: Improve School Management in State-Run Schools (under Component 2.b: Education)	LAC	Tania Dmytraczenko	2013	2015	1,050
P127245	Brazil: Strengthening Public Sector Management Technical Assistance Project	2.2: Education: Early Child Education (ECE) management system (under Component 2: Innovating in Service Provision)	LAC	Rafael Chelles Barroso	2013	2018	32.4

table continues next page

Table A.1 Database of EMIS Projects *(continued)*

Project ID	Project	EMIS components	Region	Task team leader	Approval year	Closing year	Project cost (US$, millions)
P126343	Brazil: Swap for Parana Multi-Sector Development Project	Subcomponent 2.7: Education: development of an integrated system for the management of the Borrower's school infrastructure and equipment (under Component 2: Technical Assistance for More Efficient and Effective Public Management)	LAC	Fanny Weiner	2013	2018	713.2
P117596	China: Guangdong Social Security Integration and Rural Worker Training Project	Component 1: Social Security MIS	EAP	Sun Changqing	2013	2019	149.1
P132742	Afghanistan: Second Skills Development Project	MIS system for M&E (under Component 4: Project Management, Monitoring & Evaluation and Public Awareness)	SAS	Leopold Remi Sarr	2013	2018	55
P130182	Armenia: Education Improvement Project	Subcomponent 1.3: Improving data-collection and monitoring of the education system performance (under Component 1: Enhancing the Quality of General Education)	ECA	Mario Cristian Aedo Inostroza	2014	2020	37.5
P107772	Armenia: Second Adaptable Program Lending (APL2) for the Education Quality and Relevance Project	Subcomponent 2.2: Developing a Tertiary Education Management Information System (under Component 2: Supporting Tertiary Education Reforms in the Context of Bologna Agenda)	ECA	Dandan Chen	2009	2015	31.26
P102117	Azerbaijan: Second Education Sector Development Project	Subcomponent 5.2: EMIS expansion (under Component 5: Strengthening Education Development and Management)	ECA	Dandan Chen	2008	2016	45.4
P145749	Bangladesh: Additional Financing for Higher Education Quality Enhancement Project	(i) Improving the strategic capacity of UGC (under Component 2: Building Institutional Capacity)	SAS	Yoko Nagashima	2014	NA	146.2

table continues next page

Table A.1 Database of EMIS Projects *(continued)*

Project ID	Project	EMIS components	Region	Task team leader	Approval year	Closing year	Project cost (US$, millions)
P146255	Bangladesh: Additional Financing for Secondary Education Quality and Access Enhancement Project	Subcomponent 3.2: Institutional Capacity Building (under Component 3: Institutional Capacity Strengthening), Monitoring and Evaluation (under Component 4: Monitoring and Evaluation)	SAS	Dilip Parajuli	2014	NA	280
P106216	Bangladesh: Higher Education Quality Enhancement Project	Subcomponent 2.1: Improving the Strategic Capacity of UGC (under Component 2: Building Institutional Capacity)	SAS	Yoko Nagashima	2009	2019	91.5
P131394	Bangladesh: Second Reaching Out-of-School Children Project	Subcomponent 4.1: Monitoring (under Component 4: Monitoring and Evaluation)	SAS	Dilip Parajuli	2013	2017	137.5
P106161	Bangladesh: Secondary Education Quality and Access Improvement	Subcomponent 4. I: Monitoring (under Component 4: Monitoring and Evaluation)	SAS	Dilip Parajuli	2009	2018	155.7
P090807	Bangladesh: Skills and Training Enhancement Project	(b) Development and management of a Human Resource Management Information System (HRMIS) (under Component 3: Institutional Capacity Development)	SAS	Md. Mokhlesur Rahman	2010	2016	88
P113435	Bangladesh: Third Primary Education Development Program (PEDPIII)	Monitoring and Evaluation (M&E) (under component Improving Program Planning and Management, and Strengthening Institutions)	SAS	Ayesha Y. Vawda	2012	2016	5,860
P107146	Brazil: Acre Social and Economic Inclusion and Sustainable Development Project	Subcomponent 2.1: Expansion and improvement of quality of basic education services (under Component 2: Social and Economic Inclusion in Rural Areas)	LAC	Adriana Goncalves Moreira	2009	2020	150

table continues next page

Table A.1 Database of EMIS Projects *(continued)*

Project ID	Project	EMIS components	Region	Task team leader	Approval year	Closing year	Project cost (US$, millions)
P126372	Brazil: Recife Swap Education and Public Management Project	Subcomponent 2(c): Public debt management (under Component 2: Strengthen Institutions for More Efficient and Effective Public Management)	LAC	Michael Drabble	2012	2018	890.5
P120830	Brazil: Sector-Wide Approach (SWAp) to Strengthen Public Investment Project	A8: Development and implementation of a contract management information system (under Sector 4: Public Sector Management)	LAC	Thomas Kenyon	2012	2017	903.5
P106605	Cambodia: Higher Education Quality and Capacity Improvement Project	(a) Strengthen the HE Management Information System (HEMIS) (under Component 4: Project Management and Monitoring and Evaluation)	EAP	Tsuyoshi Fukao	2011	2016	23
P117107	China: Liaoning and Shandong Technical and Vocational Education and Training Project	Subcomponent 2.1: Conduct of monitoring, evaluation, and policy studies (under Component 2: Knowledge Development, Policy Studies and Capacity Building)	EAP	Liping Xiao	2010	2016	74.43
P123146	Costa Rica: Higher Education Improvement Project	Subcomponent 2.2: Developing the Labor Market Observatory and the public higher education information system (under Component 2: Strengthening Institutional Capacity for Quality Enhancement)	LAC	Marcelo Becerra	2013	2018	249.1
P123315	Djibouti: Strengthening Institutional Capacity and Management of the Education System	Subcomponent 1.1: Improving management and accountability (under Component 1: Reinforcing Institutional Capacity and Performance of the Education System)	MNA	Karine M. Pezzani	2012	2018	6

table continues next page

Table A.1 Database of EMIS Projects *(continued)*

Project ID	Project	EMIS components	Region	Task team leader	Approval year	Closing year	Project cost (US$, millions)
P126364	El Salvador: Education Quality Improvement Project	Subcomponent 2.1: Strengthening of MINED's policy making, planning, implementation, and monitoring capacity (under Component 2: Improvement of MINED's Institutional Capacity and the Schooling)	LAC	Robert J. Hawkins	2012	2018	70.4
P089898	Guatemala: Education Quality and Secondary Education Project	3.a: Consolidation and Strengthening of School-Based Management for Education Quality; 3.b: Consolidation and Strengthening of Departmental Supervision and Technical Assistance to Schools (under 3: School Management in Support of Education Quality)	LAC	Juan Diego Alonso	2007	2016	80
P147924	Guyana: Secondary Education Improvement Project	Subcomponent 3.1: Design, develop, and implement a new education management information system to increase efficiency in education sector data management and information use for planning and policy making (under Component 3: Strengthen Institutional Capacity and Project Management)	LAC	Hongyu Yang	2014	2020	10
P124134	Haiti: Education for All Project in Support of the Second Phase of the Education for All Program Project	Restructure and reinforce education sector governance	LAC	Juan Baron	2012	2015	70
P102549	India: Second Technical Engineering Education Quality Improve-ment Project	Component 2.2: Project Monitoring, Evaluation, and Management (under Component 2: Improving System Management)	SAS	Andreas Blom	2010	2015	500

table continues next page

Lessons Learned from World Bank Education Management Information System Operations
http://dx.doi.org/10.1596/978-1-4648-1056-5

Table A.1 Database of EMIS Projects *(continued)*

Project ID	Project	EMIS components	Region	Task team leader	Approval year	Closing year	Project cost (US$, millions)
P144447	India: Third Elementary Education Project (SSA III)	11.4: Unified District Information System for Education (UDISE) (under Component II: Strengthening Monitoring and Evaluation for Improved Accountability)	SAS	Shabnam Sinha	2014		29,662
P099047	India: Vocational Training Improvement Project	(c) Project monitoring and dissemination of information with the help of a computer-based management information system (under Component 3: Project Management, Monitoring and Evaluation)	SAS	Nalin Jena/Hong W. Tan	2007	2015	359
P121842	Indonesia: Research and Innovation in Science and Technology Project	1(a) (iv): S&T information system (under Component 1: Improving Innovation Policy Framework and Performance of Public)	EAP	Dandan Chen	2013	2021	95
P147074	Jamaica: Additional Financing and Restructuring for the Early Childhood Development Project	(c) Updating the management information systems of the ECC and MOH to capture information from the CHDP (under Part 2: Institutional Strengthening)	LAC	Harriet Nannyonjo	2014	2015	14
P095673	Jamaica: Early Childhood Development Project	1: Evidence Based-Decision Making (under Component 1: Co-Financing the Implementation of the NSP under SWAP Modalities)	LAC	Christoph Kurowski	2008	2019	508.9
P107407	Jamaica: Education Transformation Capacity Building Project	3.3: Monitoring and Evaluation (under Project Component 3: Communications, Project Management, and Monitoring and Evaluation)	LAC	Cynthia Hobbs	2010	2015	16

table continues next page

Table A.1 Database of EMIS Projects *(continued)*

Project ID	Project	EMIS components	Region	Task team leader	Approval year	Closing year	Project cost (US$, millions)
P105036	Jordan: Second Education Reform for the Knowledge Economy	Subcomponent 2.1: Policy Development, Strategic Planning, Monitoring and Evaluation (under Component 2: Monitoring & Evaluation and Organizational Development)	MNA	Francis Peter Buckland	2009	2016	408
P113350	Kyrgyz Republic: Sector Support for Education Reform Project	Design and operationalize an automated monitoring system that incorporates key variables pertaining to school budgets, expenditures, and efficiency	ECA	Dingyong Hou	2013	2018	16.5
P145544	Lao PDR: Early Childhood Education Project	Develop the foundations for a child development monitoring system (under Component 3: Project Management, Capacity Development and Monitoring and Evaluation)	EAP	Omporn Regel/ Boun Oum Inthaxoum	2014	2020	28
P118187	Lebanon: Second Education Development Project	Subcomponent 3.2: Information for Planning and Management (Component 3: Education Sector Policy Development and Management)	MNA	Juan Manuel Moreno Olmedilla	2011	2017	42.6
P128378	Macedonia, FYR: Skills Development and Innovation Support Project	Subcomponent 1.1: Quality Assurance in Higher Education (under Component 1: Improving Transparency of Higher Education)	ECA	Bojana Naceva	2014	2019	24
P131331	Maldives: Enhancing Education Development Project (EEDP)	3.2: Project Coordination, Monitoring and Evaluation (under Component 3: Project Coordination, Monitoring and Evaluation, and Program Development)	SAS	Harsha Aturupane	2013	2018	11
P127388	Moldova: Education Reform Project	Establish a consolidated EMIS (under Component 1: Strengthening the Quality of Education)	ECA	Andrea C. Guedes	2013	2018	40

table continues next page

http://dx.doi.org/10.1596/978-1-4648-1056-5

Table A.1 Database of EMIS Projects (continued)

Project ID	Project	EMIS components	Region	Task team leader	Approval year	Closing year	Project cost (US$, millions)
P148110	Mongolia: Education Quality Reform Project	Supporting the Department of Monitoring and Evaluation of the MES to integrate student-learning outcomes into tracking of learning trends. Supporting the capacity building of the MES (under Component 4: System Management, Monitoring and Evaluation)	EAP	Prateek Tandon	2014	2020	14.9
P146332	Myanmar: Decentralizing Funding to Schools Project	Contribute to strengthening the use of data in the education system (under Component 3: Capacity Improvement to Strengthen Monitoring and Implementation of Programs)	EAP	James Stevens/ Lars Sondergaard	2014	2019	100
P125610	Nepal: Additional Financing for the School Sector Reform Program Project	Develop an integrated Education Management Information System (EMIS), integrated with Financial Management Information system, making it operational	SAS	Afrah Al-Ahmadi/ Saurav Dev Bhatta	2013	2017	4954
P104015	Nepal: Enhanced Vocational Education and Training Project	4.2: Monitoring and Evaluation (under Component 4: Project Management and Monitoring and Evaluation)	SAS	Saurav Dev Bhatta/ Sangeeta Goyal/ Venkatesh Sundararaman	2011	2016	60.9
P113441	Nepal: School Sector Reform Program Project	3.3: Program Management and Monitoring and Evaluation (under Component 3: Institutional Capacity Strengthening)	SAS	Raiendra D. Joshi/ Venkatesh Sundararaman	2010	2017	2635
P126357	Nicaragua: Second Support to the Education Sector Project	3.1: Improving and Integrating MINED's Planning and Statistical Information Systems (Component 3: Strengthening MINED's Education Management Capacity)	LAC	Michael Drabble/ Robert Hawkins	2012	2016	32.95

table continues next page

Table A.1 Database of EMIS Projects *(continued)*

Project ID	Project	EMIS components	Region	Task team leader	Approval year	Closing year	Project cost (US$, millions)
P125958	Pakistan: Second Punjab Education Sector Reforms Program (PESRP-II) Project	Monitoring and evaluation system	SAS	Dhushyanth Raju	2012	2016	4,407
P125952	Pakistan: Second Sindh Education Sector Project	Annual School Census (under I: Results-Based Component)	SAS	Umbreen Arif/ Dhushyanth Raju	2013	2017	2,600
P118779	Pakistan: Tertiary Education Support Project	(2.2) Policy design and TA (under Component II: Capacity Building, Policy Design and Monitoring and Evaluation)	SAS	Halil Dundar	2011	2016	2,015
P122194	Peru: Higher Education Quality Improvement Project	Subcomponent 2.1: Development and consolidation of an observatory of the accreditation of Peru's higher education (under Component 2: Development and Consolidation of a Higher Education Quality Assurance Information System)	LAC	Marcelo Becerra	2013	2018	52.17
P118904	Philippines: Learning, Equity, and Accountability Program Support Project	3.11: Improvement of targeting of Disadvantaged Groups in the Target Regions (under Component 3: Improvement of Program Design for Targeting Disadvantaged Groups in the Target Regions)	EAP	Lynnette de la Cruz Perez	2014	2019	300
P110733	Yemen, Rep.: Higher Education Quality Improvement Project	To foster the planning and monitoring capacity of the MoHESR (under Component 3: Institutional Capacity Development)	MNA	Ayesha Vawda/ Lianqin Wang	2010	2018	13
P113402	Sri Lanka: Higher Education for the Twenty-First Century Project	Component 4.2: Monitoring and Evaluation, Studies, Coordination and Communication (under Component 4: Human Resource Development, Monitoring and Evaluation, Studies, Coordination and Communication)	SAS	Yoko Nagashima	2010	2016	40

table continues next page

Lessons Learned from World Bank Education Management Information System Operations
http://dx.doi.org/10.1596/978-1-4648-1056-5

Table A.1 Database of EMIS Projects *(continued)*

Project ID	Project	EMIS components	Region	Task team leader	Approval year	Closing year	Project cost (US$, millions)
P132698	Sri Lanka: Skills Development Project	Component 1: Program Support to the Skills Sector Development Program	SAS	Halil Dundar	2014	2020	650
P113488	Sri Lanka: Transforming the School Education System as the Foundation of a Knowledge Hub Project	R. Strengthening monitoring (under Theme 3: Strengthening Governance and Delivery of Education Services)	SAS	Deepa Sankar	2012	2017	100
P116520	Timor-Leste: Second Chance Education Project	2.3: Upgrade Monitoring and Evaluation capacity of DNEAENF (under Component 2: Improved Quality of Service Delivery)	EAP	Stephen Close	2011	2016	5
P126408	Uruguay: Support to Uruguayan Public Schools Project	3.1: Information for Monitoring and Evaluating Project Activities (under Component 3: Monitoring, Evaluation and Project Management)	LAC	Diego Ambasz/ Peter A. Holland	2013	2017	73.8
P110693	Vietnam: New-Model Universities Project	1.5: Management and operational systems (Component 1: Policy and Regulatory Framework)	EAP	Mai Th. Thanh	2010	2018	200.6
P117393	Vietnam: School Readiness Promotion Project	2.1: Strengthening Planning and Reporting Systems (under Component 2: National Early Childhood Education Policy Development and Capacity Building)	EAP	Christian Bodewig/ James Stevens	2013	2017	100
P130853	Yemen, Rep.: Second Basic Education Development Project	Subcomponent 3.2: Education Management Information System (EMIS) (under Component 3: Institutional Capacity Development)	MNA	Kamel Braham	2013	2019	72
P147244	Mexico: Third Upper Secondary Education Development Policy Loan Project	Design and implementation of the whole Mexican Education Evaluation System	LAC	Peter A. Holland/ Rafael E. de Hoyos	2014	2016	601

table continues next page

Table A.1 Database of EMIS Projects *(continued)*

Project ID	Project	EMIS components	Region	Task team leader	Approval year	Closing year	Project cost (US$, millions)
P128891	Ethiopia: Third Phase of the Promoting Basic Services Project	(B3) Managing for Results (under Sub-Program B: Strengthening Local Accountability and Transparency Systems)	SSA	Qaiser M. Khan	2013	2018	4,887
P132617	Chad: Second Phase of the Education Sector Reform Project	3.2: Monitoring and Evaluation (under Component 3: Project Management, Monitoring and Evaluation)	SSA	Marie-Helene Cloutier	2013	2018	15
P128628	Congo, Rep.: Skills Development for Employability Project	Component 2: Strengthen the Technical, Planning, Implementation, and Monitoring and Evaluation Capacity of METPFQE	SSA	Celine Gavach	2013	2018	n.a.
P106855	Ethiopia: General Education Quality Improvement Program Project	Subcomponent 4.3: Education Management Information Systems (EMIS) (under Component 4: Management and Administration Program)	SSA	Thanh Thi Mai	2009	2017	417.3
P133079	Gambia, The: Results for Education Achievement and Development Project	Subcomponent 3.2: Institutional support and capacity building (under Component 3: Technical and Institutional Support)	SSA	Nathalie Lahire	2014	2018	34.8
P145741	Ghana: Secondary Education Improvement Project	Web-based school monitoring (under Component 2: Management, Research and Monitoring and Evaluation)	SSA	Deborah Newitter Mikesell	2014	2019	156
P118112	Ghana: Skills and Technology Development Project	Subcomponent 1.1: Development of COTVET technical capacity, strategic systems, and policies (under Component 1 (Part A): Institutional Strengthening of Skills Development)	SSA	Peter Darvas	2011	2016	70

table continues next page

Table A.1 Database of EMIS Projects *(continued)*

Project ID	Project	EMIS components	Region	Task team leader	Approval year	Closing year	Project cost (US$, millions)
P114847	Malawi: Improve Education Quality Project	Subcomponent 3.1: Support Teacher Management Reform (under Component III: Improve Management Capacity at All Levels)	SSA	Deepa Sankar	2010	2015	256
P131660	Malawi: Skills Development Project	Developing monitoring and evaluation systems and piloting new monitoring tools (under Component 2: Technical Assistance for System Strengthening and Policy Reforms)	SSA	Deepa Sankar	2014	2019	n.a.
P124729	Mozambique: Additional Financing for the Early Child Development Project	Adding ECD to main EMIS through capacity-building activities	SSA	Fadila Caillaud	2012	n.a.	n.a.
P125127	Mozambique: Education Sector Support Project	Subcomponent 4.1: Continuing the consolidation of the reforms in the areas of financial management and procurement as well as planning budgeting and monitoring (under Component 4: Strengthening Management of the Education Sector Administrative System)	SSA	Fadila Caillaud	2011	2015	161
P126049	Niger: Skills Development for Growth Project	Subcomponent 3.2: Monitoring and Evaluation (under Component 3: Institutional Capacity Strengthening and Monitoring and Evaluation)	SSA	Kirsten Maigaard	2013	2019	30
P123353	Nigeria: First Edo State Growth and Employment Support Credit Program	Piloting of Education Information Management Information Systems (EMIS)	SSA	Joseph-Raji/ Gloria Aitalohi	2012	2014	75
P122124	Nigeria: State Education Program Investment Project	Educational development (under Component 2: Technical Assistance)	SSA	Irajen Appasamy	2013	2017	1,342

table continues next page

Lessons Learned from World Bank Education Management Information System Operations
http://dx.doi.org/10.1596/978-1-4648-1056-5

Table A.1 Database of EMIS Projects *(continued)*

Project ID	Project	EMIS components	Region	Task team leader	Approval year	Closing year	Project cost (US$, millions)
P121455	Nigeria: State Employment and Expenditures for Results Project	B.5: State Integrated Financial Management Information Systems (SIFMIS) (under Component B: Public Financial Management Reforms)	SSA	Jens Kromann Kristensen	2012	2017	200
P150828	São Tomé and Príncipe: Additional Financing for the Quality Education for All Project	Scale up the planned development of the EMIS by providing additional computers to schools and central-level structures and by ensuring Internet connectivity between schools and the central level	SSA	Atou Seck	2014	n.a.	3.5
P146877	São Tomé and Príncipe: Second Phase of Quality Education for All Project	Subcomponent 2.1: Development of a Management Information System (under Component 2: Strengthening Management of Human Resources in the Education Sector)	SSA		2013	2017	2
P133333	Senegal: Quality and Equity of Basic Education	Provide training on how to manage a district level EMIS as well as collecting, inputting, analyzing, and reporting results to inform policy making	SSA		2013	2018	217.7
P123673	Senegal: Tertiary Education Governance and Financing for Results Project	Subcomponent 1.3: Development of a Monitoring and Evaluation system (under Component 1: Strengthening the Governance of the Tertiary Education System)	SSA		2011	2016	127.3
P098496	Tanzania: Science and Technology Higher Education Project	Component 2B: Investments in System-Wide ICT and Libraries	SSA		2008	2016	100
P114866	Tanzania: Second Secondary Education Development Program Project	Expansion of the EMIS currently under development (under Component 4: Providing Capacity Building and Technical Assistance to Implement Reforms)	SSA		2010	2015	469.3

table continues next page

Table A.1 Database of EMIS Projects *(continued)*

Project ID	Project	EMIS components	Region	Task team leader	Approval year	Closing year	Project cost (US$, millions)
P122700	Angola: Learning for All Project	Component 2: Establishing a System for Student Assessment	SSA		2013	2018	80
P129828	Ethiopia: Second Phase of General Education Quality Improvement Project	Subcomponent 4.3: Education Management Information Systems (under Component 4: Management and Capacity Building, Including EMIS)	SSA		2013	2018	550
P121805	Afghanistan: Additional Financing for Strengthening of Higher Education Project	Design of Quality Accreditation and Assurance System Financing of the National Entrance Exam (for students) and of initial improvement to MIS for processing entrance examination	SAS	Habibullah Wajdi	2010	NA	20
P083964	Afghanistan: Education Quality Improvement Program	Component 3.2: Monitoring and Evaluation (under Component 3: Policy Development and Monitoring and Evaluation)	SAS	Samantha de Silva	2005	2009	35
P078933	Albania: Education Excellence and Equity Project	Component 1: Strengthening Leadership, Management and Governance of the Education System	ECA	Keiko Inoue	2006	2013	75
P069120	Albania: Education Reform Project	Component 2. Education Management Information System	ECA	Peter Darvas	2000	2005	14.88
P095514	Argentina: Lifelong Learning and Training Project	(1) Installation of an integrated management information system (MIS) (under D: The Strengthen Management Information System, Project Administration and Studies Component)	LAC	Marcela Ines Salvador	2007	2014	678.7

table continues next page

Table A.1 Database of EMIS Projects (continued)

Project ID	Project	EMIS components	Region	Task team leader	Approval year	Closing year	Project cost (US$, millions)
P070963	Argentina: Rural Education Improvement (PROMER) Project	Subcomponent B2: Supporting the development and implementation of a system of data collection, analysis, dissemination, and use of information for policy decisions at the national level (under Component B: Enhancing the Stewardship Capacity of National Government)	LAC	Diego Ambasz	2006	2014	150
P074503	Armenia: An Education Quality and Relevance Project	Component 4: System Management and Efficiency	ECA	Meskerem Mulatu	2004	2010	20.6
P008281	Armenia: Education Financing and Management Reform Project	A. The Strategy for Finance and Management Reforms (under Component II: Capacity Building for Reform Management (US$4.4 million appraisal estimate)	ECA	Kari L. Hurt	1998	2003	20.7
P070989	Azerbaijan: Education Sector Development Project	Subcomponent 2: Establishment of Education Management Information System (EMIS) (under Component 4: Management, Planning, and Monitoring Capacity)	ECA	Juan Manuel Moreno Olmedilla	2003	2010	22.61
P044876	Bangladesh: Female Secondary School Assistance Project	MIS database (under Component 3: Strengthening Management, Accountability and Monitoring)	SAS	Irajen Appasamy	2002	2008	127.3
P050752	Bangladesh: Post-Literacy and Continuing Education for Human Development	Subcomponent 4.1: Systems Improvement (under Component 4: Strengthening Institutional Capacity)	SAS	Mark F. LaPrairie	2001	2008	48.6

table continues next page

Lessons Learned from World Bank Education Management Information System Operations
http://dx.doi.org/10.1596/978-1-4648-1056-5

Table A.1 Database of EMIS Projects *(continued)*

Project ID	Project	EMIS components	Region	Task team leader	Approval year	Closing year	Project cost (US$, millions)
P009550	Bangladesh: Primary Education Development Project	Subcomponents 2.1: Strengthening institutional capacity at the national level (under Component 2: Strengthening Institutional Capacity and Management)	SAS	Hena G. Mukherjee	1998	2004	129.1
P077789	Bangladesh: Programmatic Education Sector Adjustment Credit	Monitoring and Evaluation: Enhancing capacity of BANBEIS, dissemination of information on school quality	SAS	Amit Dar	2005	2005	100
P084567	Bangladesh: Second Programmatic Education Sector Development Support Credit Project	Monitoring and Evaluation: Enhancing capacity of BANBEIS, dissemination of information on school quality	SAS	Amit Dar	2006	2007	100
P074966	Bangladesh: The Second Primary Education Development Project	EMIS capacity (under Component 1: Quality Improvement through Organizational Development and Capacity Building Including Program Management and Monitoring and Evaluation)	SAS	Helen J. Craig	2004	2011	150
P006204	Bolivia: Education Quality and Equity Strengthening Project	Information subsystem (under Component B: Institutional Strengthening)	LAC	Patricia Alvarez	1998	2007	125.3
P083965	Bolivia: Secondary Education Transformation Project for the Municipality of La Paz	(i) Management and monitoring information system (under Component 3: Education Management and Institutional Strengthening)	LAC	Patricia Alvarez	2008	2013	10
P058512	Bosnia and Herzegovina: Education Development Project	Component 3: An Education Management Information System	ECA	Zorica Lesic	2000	2005	14.43

table continues next page

Lessons Learned from World Bank Education Management Information System Operations
http://dx.doi.org/10.1596/978-1-4648-1056-5

Table A.1 **Database of EMIS Projects** *(continued)*

Project ID	Project	EMIS components	Region	Task team leader	Approval year	Closing year	Project cost (US$, millions)
P079226	Bosnia and Herzegovina: Education Restructuring Project	Extension of education management information system (under Component 2: Education Finance and Management)	ECA	Zorica Lesic	2005	2010	0
P059565	Brazil: Bahia Education Project	(3.2) Institutional strengthening of educational management (under Component 3: Strengthening Educational Management)	LAC	Andrea C. Guedes	2001	2003	113.7
P082523	Brazil: Human Development Technical Assistance Project	Designing and developing a Ministry-wide information system to track and monitor key programs (under Component 2: Strengthening Monitoring and Evaluation in the Education Sector)	LAC	Michele Gragnolati	2005	2010	8.927
P069934	Brazil: Pernambuco Integrated Development: Education Quality Improvement	3.2 Strengthening and Modernizing Education Management (under Component 3: Supporting the State Reform)	LAC	Ricardo Rocha Silveira	2005	2010	51.23
P050762	Brazil: School Improvement Project (Fundescola I)	Strengthening national education information systems and programs (under Component 4: Strengthening Education Management and Project Administration)	LAC	Robin S. Horn	1998	2001	138.7
P050763	Brazil: Second School Improvement Program—Fundescola II	Component 4: Strengthening National Education Information Systems and Programs	LAC	Andrea C. Guedes	1999	2006	414.5

table continues next page

Lessons Learned from World Bank Education Management Information System Operations
http://dx.doi.org/10.1596/978-1-4648-1056-5

Table A.1 Database of EMIS Projects *(continued)*

Project ID	Project	EMIS components	Region	Task team leader	Approval year	Closing year	Project cost (US$, millions)
P055158	Bulgaria: Education Modernization Project	(2.3) Establishment of a General Education Management Information System (GEMIS) in the MES at the secondary level (under Component 2: Create Conditions for Improving Overall Resource Management in Primary and Secondary Schools), (3.2) Establishment of a Higher Education Management Information System (HEMIS) in the MES (under Component 3: Create Conditions for Improving Overall Resource Management in Higher Education Institutions), Component 5: Create a Competitive Teaching and Management System for Higher Education (CTMSHE) for Improving Teaching and Resource Management, Component 6: Strengthen MES Internal Management Capacity for Project Management and Communications	ECA	Reema Nayar	2001	2004	6.05
P055481	Chile: Higher Education Improvement Project	A2: Policy and Institutional Capacity Building (under Project Component A: Policy Framework and Capacity Building)	LAC	Kristian Thorn	1999	2005	278.2
P068271	Chile: Lifelong Learning and Training Project	(b) Establishing lifelong learning and training information systems (MISs) (under Establishing Instruments to Support the Provision of a Lifelong Learning and Training Services)	LAC	Dena Ringold	2002	2010	218.5

table continues next page

Table A.1 **Database of EMIS Projects** *(continued)*

Project ID	Project	EMIS components	Region	Task team leader	Approval year	Closing year	Project cost (US$, millions)
P077757	Colombia: A Cundinamarca Education Quality Improvement	(a) Strengthening of administrative, financial, and management systems of municipal schools through the provision of technical assistance, training, tailored-made internships, sharing of good practices, and acquisition of equipment (under Component A: Improving School Management to Enhance Education Quality and Relevance)	LAC	Martha Laverde	2004	2008	2.71
P074138	Colombia: Higher Education-Improving Access	Strengthening of the National Information System for Higher Education (SNIES) to provide better system-wide information for stakeholder decision making (under Component 3: Institutional Strengthening)	LAC	Alejandro Caballero	2003	2009	460
P046112	Colombia: Pasto Education Project	Promoting the consolidation of an efficient Education Information System as a management tool (under Project Component 2: Institutional Strengthening)	LAC	Martha Laverde	1998	2004	10.9
P057857	Costa Rica: Equity and Efficiency of Education Project	The development and implementation of an education sector information system at the school level (under Component 3: Improving MEP's Institutional Efficiency)	LAC	Marcelo Becerra	2005	2014	44.2
P086671	Croatia: Education Sector Development Project	Support developing policies, activities and structures (under Priority 2: Improving Monitoring and Evaluation)	ECA	Ivan Drabek	2006	2012	89.55

table continues next page

Lessons Learned from World Bank Education Management Information System Operations
http://dx.doi.org/10.1596/978-1-4648-1056-5

Table A.1 Database of EMIS Projects *(continued)*

Project ID	Project	EMIS components	Region	Task team leader	Approval year	Closing year	Project cost (US$, millions)
P086994	Djibouti: Second School Access and Improvement Program Project	Subcomponent 2.4: Learning Assessment (under Component 2: Quality Improvement)	MNA	Christina D. Wright	2006	2012	10.3
P121778	Dominican Republic: Second Performance and Account-ability of Social Sectors Development Policy Loan Program	Improving EMIS's ability to provide information to verify education conditions for Conditional Cash Transfers	LAC	Carine Clert	2011	2012	150
P125806	Dominican Republic: Third Performance and Account-ability of Social Sectors (PASS3) Development Policy Loan (DPL) Program	Establishing an integral system of monitoring and evaluation (under Policy area 1: Enhancing the Performance of Social Sector Agencies to Promote Equitable Access to Human Capital)	LAC	Aline Coudouel	2012		70
P087831	Ecuador: Support for the Strategy of Inclusion and Quality Education Project	Improved Human Resources Management (under Component 1: Providing Technical Assistance to MEC)	LAC	Livia M. Benavides	2007	2011	43
P055173	Georgia: Education System Realignment and Strength-ening Program	Development and implementation of an effective and reliable EMIS (under Component B: Strength-ening Capacity for Policy and Management)	ECA	Richard R. Hopper	2001	2008	36.13
P077759	Grenada: (OECS) Education Development Program	Expanding the Education Management Information System (EMIS) (under Component 3: Improved Governance and Management of the Education Sector)	LAC	Harriet Nannyonjo	2003	2011	2.36

table continues next page

Table A.1 Database of EMIS Projects *(continued)*

Project ID	Project	EMIS components	Region	Task team leader	Approval year	Closing year	Project cost (US$, millions)
P048652	Guatemala: Universalization of Basic Education Project	Development of the National Cultural Resources Information System (NCRIS) (under Component 3: Cultural Diversity and Pluralism) Continued Development and Updating of an Education Management Information System (EMIS) (under Component 4: Decentralization and Modernization)	LAC	Martha Laverde	2001	2009	87.24
P099918	Haiti: First Phase of the Education for All Project: Adaptable Program Lending	Component 3: Improving Institutional Governance of MENFP and the Education Sector (Establishment of an adequate MIS system for tracking all per student subsidies and school grants)	LAC	Patrick Philippe Ramanantoanina	2007	2012	38.19
P007397	Honduras: Community-Based Education Project	Support the design and implementation of an information system for the programs financed by the Project (PROHECO, Multicultural Bilingual Education—EIB and Preschool Centers—CCPREB) (under Component 4: Strengthening of Institutional Support for Community Participation and School-Based Management Program)	LAC	Andrea C. Guedes	2001	2008	53.03
P101218	Honduras: Education Quality, Governance and Institutional Strengthening Project	(3.1) Information for improved performance and greater accountability (under Component 3: Governance and Institutional Strengthening of the Ministry of Education)	LAC	Juan Diego Alonso	2008	2013	16.29

table continues next page

Lessons Learned from World Bank Education Management Information System Operations
http://dx.doi.org/10.1596/978-1-4648-1056-5

Table A.1 Database of EMIS Projects *(continued)*

Project ID	Project	EMIS components	Region	Task team leader	Approval year	Closing year	Project cost (US$, millions)
P039449	Hungary: Higher Education Reform Project	Management Information Systems component	ECA	Mary Canning	1998	2002	7.29
P072123	India: Technical/ Engineering Education Quality Improvement Project	Component 2: System Management Capacity Improvement (Establishing EMIS)	SAS	Andreas Blom	2002	2009	315.1
P045050	India: Rajasthan District Primary Education Project	To monitor project implementation, carrying out evaluation studies by third party, carrying out sample surveys and classroom observation studies, and putting in place functional Education Management Information System (EMIS) and Project Management Information System (PMIS). (under Component C/3: (c) Improving State and District Capacity to Manage Primary Education)	SAS	Prema Clarke	1999	2005	109
P055455	India: Rajasthan Second District Primary Education Project	Institutional Capacity (under Project Component 3: Building Capacity to Manage Primary Education at the State, District, and Local Levels)	SAS	Nalin Jena	2001	2008	74.4
P102547	India: Second Elementary Education Project (AFR II)	Component 1: Improving Quality with Equity (capacity building, monitoring, and evaluation)	SAS	Deepa Sankar	2008	2013	600
P050658	India: Third Technical Education Project	(c) Instituting computer-based project and financial management systems (under (iii) Efficiency Improvement)	SAS	Shashi K. Shrivastava	2001	2007	83.41

table continues next page

Table A.1 Database of EMIS Projects *(continued)*

Project ID	Project	EMIS components	Region	Task team leader	Approval year	Closing year	Project cost (US$, millions)
P097104	Indonesia: Better Education through Reformed Management and Universal Teacher Upgrading Project (BERMUTU)	Subcomponent 4.1: Monitoring of project activities and teacher certification (under Component 4: Improving Program Coordination, Monitoring, and Evaluation)	EAP	Susiana Iskandar	2008	2014	137.3
P085374	Indonesia: Managing Higher Education for Relevance and Efficiency Project	Subcomponent 1.1: Modernization of higher education sector oversight and management (under Component 1: Higher Education Reform and Oversight)	EAP	Ratna Kesuma	2005	2013	73.12
P039644	Indonesia: West Java Basic Education Project	School Mapping	EAP	Mae Chu Chang	1998	2005	124.4
P096234	Iraq: Third Emergency Education Project	Strengthening the planning and management capacity of MoE and DoEs (under Component 1: Educational Infrastructure)	MNA	Amira Mohamed Ibrahim Kazem	2006	2014	100
P071589	Jamaica: Reform of Secondary Education Project II	Development of an education management information system (EMIS) (under Component 4: Institutional Strengthening)	LAC	Cynthia Hobbs	2003	2010	16.5
P100534	Jordan: Employer-Driven Skills Development Project	Enhance information systems (under Component 1: E-TVET System and Council Development)	MNA	Juan Manuel Moreno Olmedilla	2008	2014	4.3
P069326	Jordan: Higher Education Development Project	Subcomponent 1.1: System-Wide Support (under Component 1: Initiate Improvements in Quality, Relevance, and Efficiency)	MNA	Adriana Jaramillo	2000	2007	41.83
P102487	Jordan: Higher Education Reform for Knowledge Economy Project	Component 2: Modernize Governance, Accountability, and Management Systems	MNA	Ghassan N. Alkhoja	2009		0

table continues next page

Lessons Learned from World Bank Education Management Information System Operations
http://dx.doi.org/10.1596/978-1-4648-1056-5

Table A.1 **Database of EMIS Projects** *(continued)*

Project ID	Project	EMIS components	Region	Task team leader	Approval year	Closing year	Project cost (US$, millions)
P069516	Kosovo: Education and Health Project	Subcomponent 1.1: Developing Education Funding and Management Systems and Subcomponent 1.4: Developing Education Governance and Management Structures (under Project Component 1: Education)	ECA	Betty Hanan	2000	2004	4.41
P102174	Kosovo: Institutional Development for Education Project	Providing training and an enabling operational environment for the use of the EMIS for analysis of key policy issues and decision making by MEST and municipalities (under Building Institutions and Management Capacities to Promote Quality Improvements in Primary and Secondary Education)	ECA	Flora Kelmendi	2008	2014	10
P078113	Lao PDR: A Second Education Development Project	Strengthening information systems to support improved collection, analysis, reporting, filing, storing, and maintenance of data and information (under Component C: Strengthen Capacities for Policy Analysis and Management)	EAP	Boun Oum Inthaxoum	2004	2014	29.87
P118494	Lao PDR: Additional Financing for the Second Education Development Project	Component C (Strengthen Capacities for Policy Analysis and Management, Including Project Management): Update of EMIS Strategy and Implementation Plan	EAP	Suhas D. Parandekar	2010		15.5
P049172	Latvia: Education Improvement Project	B.5. Institutional Capacity Building (under Component B: Education Quality)	ECA	Ana Maria Parchuc de Jeria Figueroa	1999	2005	39.76

table continues next page

Table A.1 **Database of EMIS Projects** (continued)

Project ID	Project	EMIS components	Region	Task team leader	Approval year	Closing year	Project cost (US$, millions)
P045174	Lebanon: General Education Project	1.1 Education information management and planning (under Original Component 1: Management and Institutional Development)	MNA	Juan Manuel Moreno Olmedilla	2000	2010	43.2
P038687	Lebanon: Vocational and Technical Education Project	Development of a Vocational Education Management Information System (EMIS) (under Component 1: VTE Policy Planning and Management)	MNA	Bassam Ramadan	1998	2004	21.6
P070112	Lithuania: Education Improvement Project	Subcomponent 1.2: Education Quality Management (under Component 1: Quality Learning)	ECA	Nina Arnhold	2002	2007	64.95
P066157	Macedonia, FYR: An Education Modernization Project	Subcomponent 2.2: Education Management Information Systems (EMIS) (under Component 2: Capacity Building for Decentralized Education)	ECA	Bojana Naceva	2004	2011	20.73
P058681	Malaysia: Education Sector Support Project	Subcomponent 3.1: Improve the Borrower's existing Education Management Information System (EMIS) (under Component 3: Institutional Strengthening)	EAP	Omporn Regel	1999	2005	244
P055944	Maldives: Third Education and Training Project	Providing technical assistance to develop an Education Management Information System (EMIS) (under (c) Strengthen Institutional Capacity)	SAS	Venita Kaul	2000	2007	17.6
P040199	Mexico: Basic Education Development (PAREIB) Project	Strengthening the national evaluation system (under Component B: Strengthening Institutional Capacity at Federal and State Levels)	LAC	Venita Kaul	1998	2002	214.5

table continues next page

Lessons Learned from World Bank Education Management Information System Operations
http://dx.doi.org/10.1596/978-1-4648-1056-5

Table A.1 **Database of EMIS Projects** *(continued)*

Project ID	Project	EMIS components	Region	Task team leader	Approval year	Closing year	Project cost (US$, millions)
P057531	Mexico: Basic Education Development Phase II	2.2 Consolidation of the national school mapping system and use in regional planning at state level (under Component 2: Strengthening Institutional Capacity at Federal and State Levels)	LAC	Harry Anthony Patrinos	2002	2004	300
P115347	Mexico: School-Based Management Project (APL2)	Component: Monitoring and Oversight (Maintenance and Upgrading of National Management Information Systems)	LAC	Rafael E. De Hoyos Navarro	2010	2014	220
P088728	Mexico: School-Based Management (APL) Project	Subcomponent 2.1: Program monitoring would finance the continuous operation, maintenance and upgrading of the PEC national management information system (under Component 2: Program Monitoring and Oversight)	LAC	Ricardo Rocha Silveira	2006	2010	240
P085593	Mexico: Tertiary Education Student Assistance Project	Subcomponent 1.2: Development of a national regulatory framework for tertiary education student assistance (under Component 1)	LAC	Erik A. Bloom	2006	2012	289.9
P084597	Montenegro: Education Reform Project	Developing EMIS	ECA	Nina Arnhold	2005	2009	5.34
P040612	Nepal: Basic and Primary Education Project	Develop information systems and skills to manage a decentralized school system (under Component 1: Strengthening Institutional Capacity)	EAP	Rajendra Dhoj Joshi	1999	2005	70.33

table continues next page

Table A.1 Database of EMIS Projects *(continued)*

Project ID	Project	EMIS components	Region	Task team leader	Approval year	Closing year	Project cost (US$, millions)
P090967	Nepal: Second Higher Education Project	Strengthening of the EMIS system (under Component 3: Higher Secondary Education): develop a computerized Education Management Information System (EMIS) (under Component 4: Strengthening System Capacity)	SAS	Mohan Prasad Aryal	2007	2014	80
P078990	Nicaragua: Education Project (PASEN)	(b) Provision of a technological platform for the establishment of the National Management Information System (SNIGI) at central and departmental levels (under Component 1: Institutional Strengthening of Management Capacities of the MINED	LAC	Michael Drabble	2005	2011	15.66
P050613	Nicaragua: Second Basic Education Project	Supporting the design and implementation of a supervision system (under Component 3: Institutional Strengthening and Modernization)	LAC	Suhas D. Parandekar	2000	2005	59.8
P100846	Pakistan: First Sindh Education Sector Development Policy Credit Project	Improve education sector management	SAS	Reema Nayar	2007	2008	100
P102607	Pakistan: Higher Education Support Program	Widening the use of a Higher Education Management Information System (HEMIS) (under d) Governance and Management)	SAS	Naveed Hassan Naqvi	2010	2010	100

table continues next page

Lessons Learned from World Bank Education Management Information System Operations
http://dx.doi.org/10.1596/978-1-4648-1056-5

Table A.1 Database of EMIS Projects *(continued)*

Project ID	Project	EMIS components	Region	Task team leader	Approval year	Closing year	Project cost (US$, millions)
P037834	Pakistan: Northern Education Project	(b) Improving the information base for planning and management decisions through the conduct of baseline studies, rationalizing information flows, and developing information management systems at the local level (under 3: Strengthening Institutional Capacity)	SAS	Ameer Hussein Naqvi	1998	2004	31.89
P083228	Pakistan: Punjab Education Reform Program	Education Sector Reforms to strengthen monitoring and evaluation in order to gauge education performance outcomes and to use these to improve and readjust education policies	SAS	Tahseen Sayed Khan	2004		0
P097636	Pakistan: Second Education Sector Development Policy Credit–Punjab Province–Project	Education Sector Reforms to strengthen monitoring and evaluation in order to gauge education performance outcomes and to use these to improve and readjust education policies	SAS	Tahseen Sayed Khan	2006		0
P097471	Pakistan: Second North West Frontier Province Development Policy Credit	Improving coverage and utility of EMIS (under Monitoring and Evaluation)	SAS	Harsha Aturupane	2007		0
P107300	Pakistan: Sindh Education Sector Project (SEP)	Improving education sector management	SAS	Dhushyanth Raju	2009	2012	1,911
P090346	Pakistan: Third Punjab Education Development Policy Credit	Strengthening M&E	SAS	Tahseen Sayed Khan	2006	2006	0
P106686	Panama: Basic Education Quality Improvement Project	Strengthening institutional capacity	LAC	Maria Eugenia Bonilla-Chacin	2009		0

table continues next page

Table A.1 Database of EMIS Projects *(continued)*

Project ID	Project	EMIS components	Region	Task team leader	Approval year	Closing year	Project cost (US$, millions)
P052021	Panama: Second Basic Education Project	(b) To support the then ongoing implementation of MEDUCA's management information system (under Component C: Institutional Strengthening)	LAC	Maria Eugenia Bonilla-Chacin	2001	2009	38.2
P105555	Panama: Second Basic Education Project (Additional Financing)	Component 3: Institutional Strengthening.	LAC	Maria Eugenia Bonilla-Chacin	2008		5
P073967	Romania: Rural Education Project	Component 3: Strengthen Monitoring, Evaluation and Policy Making	ECA	Mariana Doina Moarcas	2003	2009	91.88
P044614	Romania: School Rehabilitation Project	Institutional capacity improvement	ECA	Mariana Doina Moarcas	1998	2004	130
P050474	Russian Federation: Education Reform Project	Objective 3: Improving Quality and Standards	ECA	Ernesto P. Cuadra	2001	2006	123.7
P075189	Republic of Serbia Education Improvement Project	Component 3: Education Information System	ECA	Tobias Linden	2002	2007	11.05
P050741	Sri Lanka: Improving Relevance and Quality of Undergraduate Education	A. Strengthening national planning, monitoring and evaluation systems, and coordination at the national level (under Component 1. Building Institutional Capacity in the Tertiary Education System)	SAS	Yoko Nagashima	2003	2010	55.32
P010525	Sri Lanka: Second General Education Project	(c) Develop and implement an Education Management Information System (EMIS)/Financial Management System (under Component 6: Education Management and Planning)	SAS	Helen J. Craig	1997	2006	88.1
P086664	St. Vincent and the Grenadines: OECS Education Development Project	Strengthening management and governance	LAC	Harriet Nannyonjo	2004	2012	9.32

table continues next page

Lessons Learned from World Bank Education Management Information System Operations
http://dx.doi.org/10.1596/978-1-4648-1056-5

Table A.1 Database of EMIS Projects *(continued)*

Project ID	Project	EMIS components	Region	Task team leader	Approval year	Closing year	Project cost (US$, millions)
P075978	St. Kitts and Nevis: Education Development Project (OECS)	Expansion of the education management information system (EMIS) (under Component 3: Improved Governance and Management in the Education System)	LAC	Harriet Nannyonjo	2002	2009	7.77
P097141	St. Lucia: OECS Skills for Inclusive Growth Project	Development of the MIS (under Component 3: Project management and institutional strengthening)	LAC	Harriet Nannyonjo	2007	2014	5.52
P095873	Timor-Leste: Education Sector Support Project	Subcomponent 3.2: School-site selection aiming to finance the review (under Component 3: Construction/ Rehabilitation Design and Quality Assurance)	EAP	Susiana Iskandar	2007	2013	20.3
P070268	Timor-Leste: Emergency School Readiness Project	School mapping	EAP	Alfonso F. de Guzman	2001	2002	41.7
P082999	Tunisia: Education Quality Improvement Program II (EQIP)	Subcomponent B2 (Career Information and Guidance) (under Component B: Diversity in Secondary Education)	MNA	Adriana Jaramillo	2004	2011	129.7
P005741	Tunisia: Higher Education Reform Support Project	Computerizing university management information systems (under Component D: Intensified Use of New Technologies)	MNA	Linda K. English	1998	2005	79.7
P075809	Tunisia: Second Higher Education Reform Support Project	Management information systems and IT infrastructure (under Component 3: Provide Grants to Improve Academic Quality and Institutional Performance)	MNA	Karine M. Pezzani	2006	2014	60.18
P009089	Turkey: Basic Education Project	Strengthen Education Management Information Systems (under Component (3): Program Implementation Support)	ECA	Robin S. Horn	1998	2003	286.5

table continues next page

Table A.1 Database of EMIS Projects *(continued)*

Project ID	Project	EMIS components	Region	Task team leader	Approval year	Closing year	Project cost (US$, millions)
P077738	Ukraine: Equal Access to Quality Education in Ukraine Project	(ii) Development of an Education Management Information System (EMIS) (under Component 3: Efficiency and Management of Resources)	ECA	Scherezad Joya Monami Latif	2005	2010	86.59
P070937	Uruguay: Third Basic Education Quality Improvement Project	(ii) Development and implementation of Education Improvement Projects (PMEs) (under Institutional Strengthening)	LAC	Diego Ambasz	2002	2013	137.6
P004823	Vanuatu: Second Education Project	School Mapping	EAP	Ian R. Collingwood	2001		0
P004828	Vietnam: Higher Education Project	Monitoring and evaluation of higher education system	EAP	Thanh Thi Mai	1999	2008	98.75
P044803	Vietnam: Primary Education for Disadvantaged Children Project	Subcomponent 3.2: Institutional Strengthening (under Component 3: National and Provincial Institutional and Technical Support for FSQL)	EAP	Binh Thanh Vu	2003	2011	258.6
P051838	Vietnam: Primary Teacher Development	B4: Capacity Building in TTIs and in DoETs (under Component C: Quality Assurance)	EAP	Thanh Thi Mai	2002	2007	32.2
P079665	Vietnam: Second Higher Education Project	Development of HEMPIS	EAP	Thanh Thi Mai	2007	2012	63.4
P065593	West Bank and Gaza: Education Action Project	Subcomponent 1.1: Policy, Planning and Financing (under Component 1: Strengthening the MoE Capacity)	MNA	Adriana Jaramillo	2001	2006	7
P043255	Yemen, Rep.: Basic Education Expansion Project	Subcomponent 3.2: Planning, monitoring, and evaluation (under Project Component 3: Capacity Building)	MNA	Ayesha Y. Vawda	2001	2007	67.3
P076183	Yemen, Rep.: Higher Education Learning and Innovation Project	(b) Capacity building in the MHESR (under Component I: Governance)	MNA	Gillian M. Perkins	2002	2008	2.72

table continues next page

Table A.1 Database of EMIS Projects *(continued)*

Project ID	Project	EMIS components	Region	Task team leader	Approval year	Closing year	Project cost (US$, millions)
P086308	Yemen, Rep.: Second Vocational Training Project	Development of a basic management information system for TVET	MNA	Kamel Braham	2007		
P128284	Senegal: First Governance and Growth Support Credit Program	HR MIS for teacher/ nonteaching staff salaries	SSA	E. Philip English	2013	2014	55
P075964	Cameroon: Education Development Capacity Building	Improvement in the efficiency of the education sector's information system (under Strengthening the Education Information System and Planning Capacity)	SSA	Shobhana Sosale	2005	2012	22.2
P055468	Cape Verde: Education and Training Consolidation and Modernization Project	EMIS (under Component 4: Capacity Building)	SSA	Geraldo Joao Martins	1999	2004	7.4
P000527	Chad: Education Sector Reform Project	Strengthening of the Education Management Information System (EMIS) and project management (under Enhancing Institutional Capacity)	SSA	Marie-Helene Cloutier	2003	2012	107.5
P084317	Congo, Rep.: Support to Basic Education	Establishment and operationalization of an Education Management and Information System (EMIS) (under Capacity Building for Planning)	SSA	Cristina Isabel Panasco Santos	2005	2013	35
P035655	Côte d'Ivoire: Education and Training Support Project	(ii) The development and installation of an education and management information system (EMIS) (under Component 3: Developing Institutional Capacity)	SSA	Hamoud Abdel Wedoud Kamil	2002	2012	82.8

table continues next page

Table A.1 Database of EMIS Projects *(continued)*

Project ID	Project	EMIS components	Region	Task team leader	Approval year	Closing year	Project cost (US$, millions)
P086294	Congo, Dem. Rep.: Education Sector Report	(i) Strengthening SECOPE's capacity at the central and provincial level in the field of database planning and management, as well as resources management and monitoring	SSA	Dung-Kim Pham	2007	2014	150
P070272	Eritrea: Education Sector Improvement Project	(d) Introduce improved methods for school mapping (under Component 1: Increasing Equitable Enrollment in Basic Education)	SSA	Susan E. Hirshberg	2003	2012	47.6
P068463	Eritrea: Integrated Early Childhood Development Project	Monitoring and evaluation	SSA	Susan E. Hirshberg	2000	2007	51.7
P035643	Gambia, The: Third Education Sector Project	Establishing a comprehensive management and information system (under Component 9: Capacity Building for Sector Management)	SSA	Meskerem Mulatu	1998	2005	51.3
P050620	Ghana: An Education Sector Project	Education Management Information System (under Component A: Sector Capacity Building (SCB))	SSA	Peter Darvas	2004	2011	74.14
P000974	Ghana: National Functional Literacy Program	Improvement of management information systems (MIS) (under Component 4: Monitoring, Evaluation and Research Project)	SSA	Eunice Yaa Brimfah Ackwerh	1999	2006	7
P057188	Guinea: Pre-Service Teacher Education Project		SSA	Souleymane Sow	1999	2002	3.86
P087479	Kenya: Education Sector Support Project	(b) Strengthening the MoE's Education Management Information System (EMIS) (under Strengthening Sector Management)	SSA	Shobhana Sosale	2006	2010	1084

table continues next page

Lessons Learned from World Bank Education Management Information System Operations
http://dx.doi.org/10.1596/978-1-4648-1056-5

Table A.1 Database of EMIS Projects *(continued)*

Project ID	Project	EMIS components	Region	Task team leader	Approval year	Closing year	Project cost (US$, millions)
P082378	Kenya: Free Primary Education Support Project	(iii) Education management information system (under Component 2: Capacity Building)	SSA	Michael Mills	2003	2007	54.98
P056416	Lesotho: Second Education Sector Development Project	Subcomponent F: Capacity Building in Planning, Monitoring and Evaluation (under Component II: Primary and Secondary Education)	SSA	Xiaoyan Liang	1999	2003	26.7
P083326	Madagascar: Second Poverty Reduction Support Credit Project	(i) Developing a plan to strengthen the monitoring and evaluation system, (ii) elaborating a data collection system, (iii) strengthening coordination among donors (under Monitoring and Evaluation)	SSA	Benu Bidani	2005	2006	80
P040650	Mali: Education Sector Expenditure Program	Component 3: Strengthening Education System Capacity for Decentralization and Policy Monitoring	SSA	Adama Ouedraogo	2000	2007	541.2
P093991	Mali: Second Education Sector Investment Program Project	(iii) Setup of an Integrated Education Management Information System (under Strengthening Institutional Management Capacities of the Education Sector)	SSA	Pierre Joseph Kamano	2007	2010	35
P071308	Mauritania: Education Sector Development Program	Management Capacity in the Education Sector (under Component 4: Strengthening the Administrative, Financial, and Pedagogic Management Capacity in the Education Sector)	SSA	Cherif Diallo	2001	2010	49.9

table continues next page

Table A.1 Database of EMIS Projects *(continued)*

Project ID	Project	EMIS components	Region	Task team leader	Approval year	Closing year	Project cost (US$, millions)
P087180	Mauritania: Higher Education	The establishment of, and related training for, an integrated management information system (MIS) (under Component 2: Institutional Development)	SSA	Irajen Appasamy	2004	2013	6.6
P001786	Mozambique: Education Sector Strategic Program Project	(iv) Ensuring systematic monitoring and evaluation (under 3: Institutional Capacity to Strengthen Management Capacity)	SSA	Xiaoyan Liang	1999	2006	72.2
P109333	Namibia: Second Development Policy Loan in Support of the Education and Training Sector Improvement Program	Integrated Financial Management and Information Systems (IFMIS) (under component Strengthening Institutional and Management Capacity)	SSA	Tazeen Fasih	2008	2011	60.37
P061209	Niger: A Basic Education Project	Strengthening the Capacity of COGESs (under Part C: Strengthening Management Capacity at MoE and Empowerment of Local Communities)	SSA	Adama Ouedraogo	2003	2009	30
P066571	Nigeria: Second Primary Education Project	Subcomponent 1: (a) Collection, collation, and processing of information gathered under the First Primary Education project; (b) development of a comprehensive information base for decision making and for planning and monitoring of the UBE program (under Component D: Develop an Enhanced Information Base for Decision-Making for UBE)	SSA	Olatunde Adetoyese Adekola	2000	2004	61.11

table continues next page

Table A.1 **Database of EMIS Projects** *(continued)*

Project ID	Project	EMIS components	Region	Task team leader	Approval year	Closing year	Project cost (US$, millions)
P096151	Nigeria: State Education Sector Project	Subcomponent 1: Strengthening Education Management Information Systems (under Component 3: Institutional Development for Key Functions of the State Ministries of Education and LGEAs).	SSA	Olatunde Adetoyese Adekola	2007	2011	65.42
P071494	Nigeria: Universal Basic Education Project	(b) Develop Education Management Information Systems (under Provision of Support to Participating States)	SSA	Marito H. Garcia	2002	2006	59.1
P122247	Rwanda: Eighth Poverty Reduction Support Financing Project	Monitoring and Evaluation	SSA	Yoichiro Ishihara	2011	2012	125
P047319	Senegal: Quality Education for All	Implementation of a computerized, integrated School Information System	SSA	Atou Seck	2000	2005	0
P089254	Senegal: Quality Education for All Project	(ii) Strengthen M&E (under Component III. Strengthening Management, Monitoring and Communication throughout the System)	SSA	Atou Seck	2006	2012	85.6
P074320	Sierra Leone: Rehabilitation of Basic Education	Education Management Information System (under Component 2: Enhanced Institutional Capacity of the MEYS)	SSA	Eunice Yaa Brimfah Ackwerh	2003	2009	42.54
P083080	Tanzania: A Secondary Education Development Program	Improving access to and use of EMIS	SSA	Arun R. Joshi	2004	2007	250
P002789	Tanzania: Human Resources Development Pilot Project	Capacity Building by Providing Technology (under Component III: Capacity Building)	SSA	Rest Barnabas Lasway	1997	2005	24.02

table continues next page

Table A.1 Database of EMIS Projects *(continued)*

Project ID	Project	EMIS components	Region	Task team leader	Approval year	Closing year	Project cost (US$, millions)
P002972	Uganda: Education Sector Adjustment Operation	Strengthening sector management	SSA	Patrick D. Murphy	1998	2000	155
P003249	Zambia: Basic Education Subsector Investment Program	Administration and capacity-building component	SSA	Dandan Chen	1999	2006	224
P057167	Zambia: Technical Education Vocational & Entrepreneur Training (TEVET) Development Program Support Project	Component 7: Information Systems	SSA	Carlos A. Rojas	2001	2008	28.17

Note: EAP = East Asia and Pacific; ECA = Europe and Central Asia; LAC = Latin American and the Caribbean; MNA = Middle East and North Africa; SAS = South Asia; SSA = Sub-Saharan Africa.

Lessons Learned from World Bank Education Management Information System Operations
http://dx.doi.org/10.1596/978-1-4648-1056-5

Database of ID4D Projects

Table B.1 Database of ID4D Projects

Country	Project ID	Project name	Region	Global practice	Project status
Afghanistan	P082610	Emergency Public Administration Project II	SAR	GGP	Closed
Afghanistan	P099980	Public Financial Management Reform Project	SAR	GGP	Closed
Albania	P096263	Land Administration and Management Project (LAMP)	ECA	SURR	Closed
Albania	P105143	MDTF for Capacity Building and Support to Implement the Integrated Planning System	ECA	GGP	Closed
Albania	P107382	Social Service Delivery Project AF	ECA	SPL	Closed
Albania	P122233	Social Assistance Modernization Project	ECA	SPL	Active
Albania	P129332	Second MDTF for Capacity Building Support to Implement the IPS (IPS 2)	ECA	GGP	Active
Albania	P151972	Citizen-Centered Public Services	ECA	GGP	Pipeline
Antigua and Barbuda	P126791	Public and Social Sector Transformation Project (PSST)	LCR	SPL	Active
Argentina	P006029	Public Sector Reform Technical Assistance Project	LCR	GGP	Closed
Argentina	P070448	Subnational Government Public Sector Modernization Program	LCR	GGP	Closed
Argentina	P101171	Social and Fiscal National ID System II	LCR	GGP	Closed
Armenia	P111942	Tax Administration Modernization Project	ECA	GGP	Active
Armenia	P115647	E-Society and Innovation for Competitiveness (EIC) Project	ECA	T&ICT	Active
Bangladesh	P121528	Identification System for Enhancing Access to Services (IDEA) Project	SAR	GGP	Active
Bangladesh	P129770	Revenue Mobilization Program for Results: VAT Improvement Program (VIP)	SAR	GGP	Active
Bangladesh	P132634	Safety Net Systems for the Poorest Project	SAR	SPL	Active
Bangladesh	P146520	Income Support Program for the Poor	SAR	SPL	Pipeline

table continues next page

Table B.1 Database of ID4D Projects *(continued)*

Country	Project ID	Project name	Region	Global practice	Project status
Bolivia	P006160	Public Financial Management Project	LCR	GGP	Closed
Brazil	P101504	Second Bolsa Familia	LCR	SPL	Active
Burkina Faso	P000301	Public Institutional Development Project	AFR	GGP	Closed
Burkina Faso	P124015	Social Safety Net Project	AFR	SPL	Active
Burundi	P078627	Economic Management Support Project	AFR	GGP	Closed
Chad	P133021	Value Chain Support Project	AFR	T&C	Active
Chile	P006669	Public Sector Management Project (2)	LCR	GGP	Closed
Chile	P069259	Public Expenditure Management Project	LCR	GGP	Closed
China	P036041	Fiscal Technical Assistance Project	EAP	GGP	Closed
Colombia	P006889	Public Financial Management Project	LCR	GGP	Closed
Colombia	P040109	Public Financial Management Project (02)	LCR	GGP	Closed
Colombia	P106628	Improving Public Management Project	LCR	GGP	Active
Congo, Dem. Rep.	P104041	Enhancing Governance Capacity	AFR	GGP	Active
Congo, Dem. Rep.	P122229	Public Service Reform and Rejuvenation Project	AFR	GGP	Active
Congo, Dem. Rep.	P145965	DRC Human Development Systems Strengthening	AFR	HNP	Active
Congo, Dem. Rep.	P147555	Health System Strengthening for Better Maternal and Child Health Results Project (PDSS)	AFR	HNP	Pipeline
Costa Rica	P148435	National Health Insurance System	LCR	HNP	Pipeline
Côte d'Ivoire	P082817	Post-Conflict Assistance Project—AF	AFR	SURR	Active
Côte d'Ivoire	P108809	Support to the Safeguard and Modernization of Civil Registry	AFR	GGP	Closed
Croatia	P102778	Revenue Administration Modernization Project	ECA	GGP	Active
Djibouti	P130328	DJ Crisis Response—Social Safety Net Project	AFR	SPL	Active
Dominica	P094869	Growth and Social Protection TA Credit	LCR	GGP	Closed
Dominican Republic	P076802	Health Reform Support (APL)	LCR	HNP	Closed
Dominican Republic	P090010	Social Sectors Investment Program	LCR	SPL	Active
Ecuador	P007136	Modernization of the State Technical Assistance Project	LCR	GGP	Closed
El Salvador	P007164	Public Sector Modernization Technical Assistance Project	LCR	GGP	Closed
El Salvador	P095314	Fiscal Management and Public Sector Performance TA Loan	LCR	GGP	Active
Ethiopia	P074020	Public Sector Capacity Building Program Support Project	AFR	GGP	Closed
Ethiopia	P148447	Ethiopia: Financial Sector Development Project	AFR	F&M	Pipeline

table continues next page

Table B.1 Database of ID4D Projects *(continued)*

Country	Project ID	Project name	Region	Global practice	Project status
Ethiopia	P150922	Ethiopia PFM Project	AFR	GGP	Pipeline
Ethiopia	P151432	Ethiopia Equitable Basic Services	AFR	SPL	Pipeline
Gambia, The	P057995	Capacity Building for Economic Management Project	AFR	GGP	Closed
Gambia, The	P132881	GM-Integrated Financial Management and Information System Project—Additional Financing	AFR	GGP	Active
Georgia	P063081	Public Sector Financial Management Reform Support	ECA	GGP	Closed
Ghana	P045588	Public Financial Management Technical Assistance Project	AFR	GGP	Closed
Ghana	P115247	Ghana—Social Opportunities Project	AFR	SPL	Active
Ghana	P144140	eTransform Ghana	AFR	T&ICT	Active
Guatemala	P066175	Integrated Financial Management III—TA Project	LCR	GGP	Closed
Guinea	P123900	Productive Social Safety Net Project	AFR	SPL	Active
Guinea	P125890	Economic Governance Project	AFR	GGP	Active
Honduras	P034607	Public Sector Modernization Technical Assistance Credit	LCR	GGP	Closed
India	P108258	e-delivery of Public Services	SAR	GGP	Closed
India	P118826	India: Bihar Integrated Social Protection Strengthening Project	SAR	SPL	Active
India	P121731	India: ICDS Systems Strengthening and Nutrition Improvement Program (ISSNIP)	SAR	HNP	Active
India	P149182	IN: Citizen Access to Responsive Services SERV SEWA Project	SAR	GGP	Pipeline
India	P150288	IN: Karnataka Panchayat Strengthening II	SAR	GGP	Pipeline
India	P150308	IN: Citizen-Centric Service Delivery Reform	SAR	GGP	Pipeline
Jamaica	P007457	Financial and Program Management Improvement Project	LCR	GGP	Closed
Jamaica	P007490	Public Sector Modernization Project	LCR	GGP	Closed
Kazakhstan	P116696	Tax Administration Reform Project (JERP)	ECA	GGP	Active
Kazakhstan	P143274	Justice Sector Institutional Strengthening Project	ECA	GGP	Active
Kenya	P066490	Public Sector Management Technical Assistance Project	AFR	GGP	Closed
Kenya	P090567	Institutional Reform and Capacity Building Technical Assistance Project	AFR	GGP	Closed
Kenya	P131305	National Safety Net Program for Results	AFR	SPL	Active
Kenya, Burundi, Madagascar	P094103	Regional Communications Infrastructure Project	AFR	T&ICT	Active
Lao PDR	P074027	Health Services Improvement Project	EAP	HNP	Active
Lao PDR	P151425	Lao PDR Health and Nutrition Program	EAP	HNP	Pipeline

table continues next page

Table B.1 **Database of ID4D Projects** *(continued)*

Country	Project ID	Project name	Region	Global practice	Project status
Liberia	P107248	Economic Governance and Institutional Reform	AFR	GGP	Active
Liberia	P109775	Public Financial Management–IFMIS	AFR	GGP	Closed
Liberia	P143064	Public Sector Modernization Project	AFR	GGP	Active
Madagascar	P149323	Social Safety Net Project	AFR	SPL	Pipeline
Malawi	P001657	Institutional Development Project (2)	AFR	GGP	Closed
Malawi	P078408	Financial Management, Transparency and Accountability Project (FIMTAP)	AFR	GGP	Closed
Malawi	P133620	Strengthening Safety Nets Systems— MASAF IV	AFR	SPL	Active
Mauritania	P082888	Public Sector Capacity Building Project	AFR	GGP	Closed
Mauritania	P146804	Governance Enhancement Project	AFR	GGP	Pipeline
Mauritania	P146804	Mauritania Public Sector Efficiency program	AFR	GGP	Pipeline
Mauritania	P150430	Mauritania Social Safety Net System	AFR	SPL	Pipeline
Mexico	P147212	MX Social Protection System	LCR	SPL	Active
Moldova	P105602	Government's Central Public Administration Reform (CPAR)	ECA	GGP	Closed
Moldova	P121231	Governance e-Transformation Project	ECA	T&ICT	Active
Moldova	P127734	Strengthening PFM and Tax Administration	ECA	GGP	Pipeline
Mongolia	P077778	Economic Capacity Building TA (ECTAP)	EAP	GGP	Closed
Montenegro	P149743	Revenue Administration Reform	ECA	GGP	Pipeline
Morocco	P125799	Judicial Performance Enhancement for Service to Citizen Project ("Mahkamati")	MNA	GGP	Active
Mozambique	P129524	Social Protection Project	AFR	SPL	Active
Myanmar	P144952	Modernization of Public Finance Management	EAP	GGP	Active
Myanmar	P145534	MM: Telecommunications Sector Reform	EAP	T&ICT	Active
Myanmar	P153113	National Community Driven Development Project	EAP	SPL	Pipeline
Nepal	P144075	National Identification Project	SAR	T&ICT	Pipeline
Nicaragua	P111795	Public Financial Management Modernization Project	LCR	GGP	Active
Nigeria	P074447	State Governance and Capacity Building Project	AFR	GGP	Closed
Nigeria	P088150	Federal Government Economic Reform and Governance Project	AFR	GGP	Closed
Nigeria	P151488	Social Protection Project	AFR	SPL	Pipeline
OECS countries	P100635	OECS E-Government for Regional Integration Program (APL)	LCR	GGP	Closed
OECS countries	P117087	OECS E-Government for Regional Integration—St. Vincent and the Grenadines (APL 2)	LCR	T&ICT	Closed
Pakistan	P036015	Improvement to Financial Reporting and Auditing Project	SAR	GGP	Closed

table continues next page

Table B.1 Database of ID4D Projects *(continued)*

Country	Project ID	Project name	Region	Global practice	Project status
Pakistan	P077306	Pakistan Tax Administration Reforms Project	SAR	GGP	Closed
Pakistan	P103160	Social Safety Net Project	SAR	SPL	Active
Pakistan	P128182	Revenue Mobilization DLI	SAR	POV	Pipeline
Pakistan	P132234	Pakistan: Punjab Public Management Reform Program	SAR	GGP	Active
Papua New Guinea	P114042	Urban Youth Employment Project	EAP	SURR	Active
Peru	P131029	PE Social Inclusion TAL	LCR	SPL	Active
Philippines	P101964	National Program Support for Tax Administration Reform	EAP	GGP	Closed
Philippines	P153446	Philippines Cross-Sectoral Public Health Enhancement Project	EAP	HNP	Pipeline
Philippines	P153744	Philippines Social Welfare Development and Reform Project II	EAP	SPL	Pipeline
Romania	P130202	Revenue Administration Modernization Project	ECA	GGP	Active
Russian Federation	P093050	Registration Project	ECA	SURR	Active
Rwanda	P149095	Rwanda Public Sector Governance Program for Results	AFR	GGP	Active
Sierra Leone	P143588	Sierra Leone Safety Nets Project	AFR	SPL	Active
South Sudan	P143915	Safety Net and Skills Development	AFR	SPL	Active
Tajikistan	P127807	Tax Administration Modernization Project	ECA	GGP	Active
Tajikistan	P130091	Private Sector Competitiveness	ECA	GGP	Active
Tanzania	P124045	Tanzania Productive Social Safety Net	AFR	SPL	Active
Timor-Leste	P092484	Planning and Financial Management Capacity Building Program	EAP	GGP	Closed
Tunisia	P144674	DTF Social Protection Reforms Support	MNA	SPL	Active
Turkey	P035759	Public Finance Management Project	ECA	GGP	Closed
Uganda	P130471	Competitiveness and Enterprise Development Project (CEDP)	AFR	T&C	Active
Uruguay	P097604	Institutions Building TAL Country	LCR	GGP	Active
Venezuela, RB	P057601	Public Expenditure Management Reform Project	LCR	GGP	Closed
Vietnam	P096418	Land Administration Project	EAP	SURR	Active
Vietnam	P099376	Tax Administration Modernization Project	EAP	GGP	Active
Vietnam	P123960	Social Assistance System Strengthening Project	EAP	SPL	Active
Vietnam	P131359	Study on e-ID Infrastructure to Improve Public Services Delivery	EAP	T&ICT	Active
Vietnam	P132776	Programmatic Social Protection AAA	EAP	SPL	Active
World	P114598	e-Id—How Secure Identification Technologies Contribute to Development	LCR	T&ICT	Closed
World	P150580	Civil Registration Vital Statistics Plan	SAR	HNP	Closed

table continues next page

Table B.1 Database of ID4D Projects *(continued)*

Country	Project ID	Project name	Region	Global practice	Project status
Yemen, Rep.	P050706	Civil Service Modernization Project	MNA	GGP	Closed
Yemen, Rep.	P101453	Institutional Reform Development Policy Grant	MNA	F&M	Closed
Yemen, Rep.	P104946	Safe Motherhood Voucher Program	MNA	HNP	Closed
Yemen, Rep.	P151923	Emergency Support to Social Protection Project	MNA	SPL	Active
Zambia	P082452	Public Sector Management Program Support Project	AFR	GGP	Closed

Note: AFR = Africa; EAP = East Asia and Pacific; ECA = Europe and Central Asia; F&M = Finance and Markets; GGP = Governance Global Practice; HNP = Health, Nutrition, and Population; LCR = Latin America and the Caribbean; MNA = Middle East and North Africa; OECS = Organisation of Eastern Caribbean States; POV = Poverty and Equity; SAR = South Asia; SPL = Social Protection and Labor; SURR = Social, Urban, Rural and Resilience; T&C = Trade and Competitiveness; T&ICT = Transport and ICT.

Bibliography

Abdul-Hamid, Husein. 2014. "What Matters Most for Education Information Systems: A Framework Paper." World Bank, Washington, DC.

Ananda, S. 2003. *Rethinking Issues of Alignment under No Child Left Behind*. San Francisco: WestEd.

Atick, Joseph J., Robert J. Palacios, Diego Angel-Urdinola, Dorothée Chen, Fatima El Kadiri El Yamani, and Ariel Pino. 2014a. "Morocco—Country Assessment: Identification for Development (ID4D)—Identification Systems Analysis." World Bank, Washington, DC. http://documents.worldbank.org/curated/en/363901472492458796/Morocco -Country-assessment-Identification-for-Development-ID4D-identification-systems -analysis.

Atick, Joseph J., Alan Harold Gelb, Seda Pahlavooni, Elena Gasol Ramos, and Zaid Safdar. 2014b. "Digital Identity Toolkit: A Guide for Stakeholders in Africa." World Bank, Washington, DC. http://documents.worldbank.org/curated/en/2014/06/20272197 /digital-identity-toolkit-guide-stakeholders-africa.

Bassett, Lucy, Gaston Mariano Blanco, and Verónica Silva Villalobos. 2010. "Management Information Systems for CCTs and Social Protection Systems in LAC: A Tool for Improved Program Management and Evidence Based-Decision Making." World Bank, Washington, DC.

Cassidy, Thomas. 2006. "Education Management Information Systems (EMIS) in Latin America and the Caribbean: Lessons and Challenges." Inter-American Development Bank, Washington, DC.

Ferrer, Guillermo. 2006. "Educational Assessment Systems in Latin America: Current Practice and Future Challenges." UNESCO, Washington, DC.

ILO (International Labour Organization). 2015. "Social Protection in Action. Building Social Protection Floors." ILO, Geneva.

Lilia, Roces Z., and Genito B. Deogracias. 2004. "Basic Education Information System (BEIS)." Department of Education, Manilla, the Philippines.

Montenegro Torres, Fernando. 2013. "Costa Rica Case Study: Primary Health Care Achievements and Challenges within the Framework of the Social Health Insurance." Universal Health Coverage (UNICO) Studies Series 14, World Bank, Washington, DC.

Nayyar-Stone, Ritu. 2013. "Using National Education Management Information Systems to Make Local Service Improvements: The Case of Pakistan." PREM Note, Special

Series on the Nuts and Bolts of M&E Systems, Poverty Reduction and Economic Management Network (PREM), World Bank, Washington, DC.

Ramírez, María-José. 2012. *Disseminating and Using Student Assessment Information in Chile.* Washington, DC: World Bank.

Severin, Eugenio. 2011. "Technologies for Education. A Framework for Action." Technical Notes 11, Inter-American Development Bank, Washington, DC.

Trucano, Michael. 2006. "Education Management Information System: A Short Case Study of Ghana." InfoDev Working Paper 4, Education, World Bank, Washington, DC.

UNESCO. 2008. "Education Management Information System in Cambodia." Regional Workshop on Education Statistics for East, West and South Asia, Bangkok, Thailand, November 9–12.

UNESCO. 2010. "Data Quality Assessment Framework (DQAF). Kenya." http://www .poledakar.com/dqaf/images/e/ee/EdDQAF-Kenya-2010-Report-Final.pdf.

World Bank. 2001a. *Implementation Completion Report. Brazil.* School Improvement Project (Fundescola I) Project, Washington, DC. http://imagebank.worldbank.org /servlet/WDSContentServer/IW3P/IB/2002/01/25/000094946_0201110404374 /Rendered/PDF/multi0page.pdf.

———. 2001b. *Implementation Completion Report. Hungary.* Higher Education Reform Project, Washington, DC. http://imagebank.worldbank.org/servlet/WDSContentServer /IW3P/IB/2001/12/17/000094946_01120404004483/Rendered/PDF/multi0page .pdf.

———. 2003a. *Implementation Completion Report. Armenia.* Education Financing and Management Reform Project, Washington, DC. http://documents.worldbank.org /curated/en/2003/06/2392710/armenia-education-financing-management -reform-project.

———. 2003b. *Implementation Completion Report. Brazil.* Bahia Education Project, Washington, DC. http://documents.worldbank.org/curated/en/2003/12/2817296 /brazil-bahia-education-project.

———. 2004a. *Implementation Completion Report. Bulgaria.* Education Modernization Project, Washington, DC. http://imagebank.worldbank.org/servlet/WDSContentServer /IW3P/IB/2004/09/30/000090341_20040930094654/Rendered/PDF/29931.pdf.

———. 2004b. *Implementation Completion Report. Lesotho.* Second Education Sector Development Project, Washington, DC. http://imagebank.worldbank.org/servlet /WDSContentServer/IW3P/IB/2004/05/07/000090341_20040507104559/Rendered /PDF/277010LES.pdf.

———. 2004c. *Implementation Completion Report. Mexico.* Basic Education Development Phase II, Washington, DC. http://imagebank.worldbank.org/servlet/WDSContentServer /IW3P/IB/2005/01/11/000160016_20050111164521/Rendered/PDF/30964.pdf.

———. 2004d. *Implementation Completion Report. Pakistan.* Northern Education Project, Washington, DC. http://imagebank.worldbank.org/servlet/WDSContentServer/IW3P /IB/2004/04/02/000012009_20040402131115/Rendered/PDF/28241.pdf.

———. 2004e. *Implementation Completion Report. Turkey.* Basic Education Project, Washington, DC. http://imagebank.worldbank.org/servlet/WDSContentServer/IW3P /IB/2004/07/01/000090341_20040701101433/Rendered/PDF/27696.pdf.

———. 2005a. *Implementation Completion Report. Albania.* Education Sector Project, Washington, DC. http://imagebank.worldbank.org/servlet/WDSContentServer/IW3P /IB/2005/06/15/000160016_20050615164242/Rendered/PDF/31861.pdf.

———. 2005b. *Implementation Completion Report. Bosnia and Herzegovina.* Education Development Project, Washington, DC. http://documents.worldbank.org/curated/en /2005/06/5854292/bosnia-herzegovina-education-development-project.

———. 2005c. *Implementation Completion Report. Latvia.* Education Improvement Project,Washington,DC.http://imagebank.worldbank.org/servlet/WDSContentServer /IW3P/IB/2005/02/16/000112742_20050216144549/Rendered/PDF/307390LV .pdf.

———. 2005d. *Implementation Completion Report. Malaysia.* Education Sector Support Project,Washington,DC.http://imagebank.worldbank.org/servlet/WDSContentServer /IW3P/IB/2005/06/17/000160016_20050617104451/Rendered/PDF/31811.pdf.

———. 2005e. *Implementation Completion Report. Nigeria.* Second Primary Education Project, Washington, DC. http://documents.worldbank.org/curated/en/2005/06 /6021830/nigeria-second-primary-education-project.

———. 2006a. *Implementation Completion Report. Brazil.* Second Improvement Program– Fundescola II, Washington, DC. http://imagebank.worldbank.org/servlet /WDSContentServer/IW3P/IB/2006/10/02/000160016_20061002120400 /Rendered/PDF/36452.pdf.

———. 2006b. *Implementation Completion Report. India.* Rajasthan District Primary Education Project, Washington, DC. http://imagebank.worldbank.org/servlet /WDSContentServer/IW3P/IB/2006/07/26/000090341_20060726095458 /Rendered/PDF/36106.pdf.

———. 2007a. *Implementation Completion Report. Bolivia.* Education Quality and Equity Strengthening Project, Washington, DC. http://imagebank.worldbank.org/servlet /WDSContentServer/IW3P/IB/2007/08/29/000020439_20070829102303 /Rendered/PDF/ICR0000546.pdf.

———. 2007b. *Implementation Completion Report. Lithuania.* Education Improvement Project, Washington, DC. http://imagebank.worldbank.org/servlet/WDSContentServer /IW3P/IB/2007/05/03/000020953_20070503113459/Rendered/PDF/ICR000091 .pdf.

———. 2007c. *Implementation Completion Report. Mali.* Education Sector Expenditure Program, Washington, DC. http://imagebank.worldbank.org/servlet/WDSContentServer /IW3P/IB/2008/08/13/000333038_20080813235108/Rendered/PDF /ICR4220REPLACE10Box334039B01PUBLIC1.pdf.

———. 2008. *Implementation Completion Report. Tanzania.* Secondary Education Development Program Project, Washington, DC. http://documents.worldbank.org /curated/en/2008/06/9718241/tanzania-secondary-education-development -program-project.

———. 2009a. *Implementation Completion Report. Afghanistan.* Education Quality Improvement Program, Washington, DC. http://imagebank.worldbank.org/servlet /WDSContentServer/IW3P/IB/2009/10/16/000350881_20091016095920/Rendered /PDF/ICR12630P0839610disclosed0101151091.pdf.

———. 2009b. *Implementation Completion Report. Guatemala.* Universalization of Basic Education Project, Washington, DC. http://documents.worldbank.org/curated/en /2009/06/10970514/guatemala-universalization-basic-education-project.

———. 2009c. *Implementation Completion Report. St. Kitts and Nevis.* Education Development Project, Washington, DC. http://imagebank.worldbank.org/servlet /WDSContentServer/IW3P/IB/2009/08/20/000333037_20090820003829 /Rendered/PDF/ICR4780P0486521C0disclosed081181091.pdf.

————. 2009d. *Implementation Completion Report. Zambia.* TEVET Development Program Support Project, Washington, DC. http://imagebank.worldbank.org/servlet /WDSContentServer/IW3P/IB/2009/08/05/000333038_20090805012206 /Rendered/PDF/ICR11020P057161IC0disclosed08131091.pdf.

————. 2010a. *Implementation Completion Report. Azerbaijan.* Education Sector Development Project, Washington, DC. http://imagebank.worldbank.org/servlet /WDSContentServer/IW3P/IB/2010/06/25/000334955_20100625015649 /Rendered/PDF/ICR11340P07098101Official0Use0Only1.pdf.

————. 2010b. *Implementation Completion Report. Brazil.* Human Development Technical Assistance Project, Washington, DC. http://imagebank.worldbank.org/servlet /WDSContentServer/IW3P/IB/2010/08/10/000334955_20100810031459 /Rendered/PDF/ICR15390P082521IC0disclosed08161101.pdf.

————. 2010c. *Implementation Completion Report. Lebanon.* General Education Project, Washington, DC. http://imagebank.worldbank.org/servlet/WDSContentServer /IW3P/IB/2010/08/10/000356161_20100810233124/Rendered/PDF /ICR14730P045171IC0disclosed08191101.pdf.

————. 2011a. *Colombia—Development Policy Loan (DPL) on Promoting an Inclusive, Equitable and Efficient Social Protection System Project.* Washington, DC. http:// documents.worldbank.org/curated/en/2011/06/14757939/colombia-development -policy-loan-dpl-promoting-inclusive-equitable-efficient-social-protection -system-project.

————. 2011b. *Implementation Completion Report. Kenya.* Education Sector Project, Washington, DC. http://imagebank.worldbank.org/servlet/WDSContentServer /IW3P/IB/2011/10/21/000386194_20111021011704/Rendered/PDF /ICR18390P087470Official0Use0Only090.pdf.

————. 2011c. *Implementation Completion Report. Ukraine.* Equal Access to Quality Education in Ukraine Project, Washington, DC. http://imagebank.worldbank.org /servlet/WDSContentServer/IW3P/IB/2011/08/09/000333038_20110809233233 /Rendered/PDF/ICR17010P077730c080801100BOX361525B.pdf.

————. 2011d. *Implementation Completion Report. Vietnam.* Primary Education for Disadvantaged Children Project, Washington, DC. http://imagebank.worldbank.org /servlet/WDSContentServer/IW3P/IB/2011/08/28/000333037_20110828234820 /Rendered/PDF/ICR15640P044800e0only0900BOX361532B.pdf.

————. 2011e. *Timor-Leste—Social Protection Administration Project.* Washington, DC. http://documents.worldbank.org/curated/en/2011/10/16569538/timor-leste-social -protection-administration-project-timor-leste-social-protection-administration-project.

————. 2012a. *Implementation Completion Report. Chad.* Education Sector Project, Washington, DC. http://imagebank.worldbank.org/servlet/WDSContentServer/IW3P /IB/2012/12/31/000333038_20121231002916/Rendered/PDF/NonAsciiFileName0 .pdf.

————. 2012b. *Implementation Completion Report. Eritrea.* Education Sector Improvement Project, Washington, DC. http://imagebank.worldbank.org/servlet/WDSContentServer /IW3P/IB/2012/03/28/000333038_20120328010002/Rendered/PDF /ICR20250P070270IC0disclosed30260120.pdf.

————. 2012c. *Implementation Completion Report. Ghana.* Education Sector Project, Washington, DC. http://documents.worldbank.org/curated/en/ 2012/04/16272475 /ghana-education-sector-project.

———. 2012d. *Implementation Completion Report. St. Vincent and the Grenadines.* OECS Education Development Project, Washington, DC. http://imagebank.worldbank.org /servlet/WDSContentServer/IW3P/IB/2012/07/30/000356161_20120730013816 /Rendered/PDF/ICR22390P086660Official0Use0Only090.pdf.

———. 2012e. *Implementation Completion Report. Vietnam.* Second Higher Education Project, Washington, DC. http://imagebank.worldbank.org/servlet/WDSContentServer /IW3P/IB/2013/05/02/000350881_20130502091923/Rendered/PDF /ICR23160P079660IC0disclosed05010130.pdf.

———. 2013. *Implementation Completion Report. Honduras.* Education Quality, Governance and Institutional Strengthening Project, Washington, DC. http:// documents.worldbank.org/curated/en/2013/12/18781658/honduras-education -quality-governance-institutional-strengthening-project-honduras-education-quality -governance-institutional-strengthening-project.

———. 2014a. *Implementation Completion Report. Argentina.* Rural Education Improvement (PROMER) Project, Washington, DC. http://imagebank.worldbank.org/servlet /WDSContentServer/IW3P/IB/2014/06/30/000442464_20140630143443 /Rendered/PDF/ICR29700P070960C0disclosed060260140.pdf.

———. 2014b. *Implementation Completion Report. Mauritania.* Higher Education Project, Washington, DC. http://documents.worldbank.org/curated/en/2014/08/20263717 /mauritania-higher-education-project.

———. 2014c. *Implementation Completion Report. Timor-Leste.* Education Sector Support Project, Washington, DC. http://imagebank.worldbank.org/servlet/WDSContentServer /IW3P/IB/2014/02/04/000350881_20140204130145/Rendered/PDF /ICR28460REVISE0IC0disclosed02040140.pdf.

———. 2015a. "EMIS Projects List." World Bank, Washington, DC. http://datatopics .worldbank.org/education/wSaber/Emis.aspx.

———. 2015b. "Identification for Development." World Bank, Washington, DC. http:// www.worldbank.org/en/topic/governance/brief/identification-for-development.

———. 2015c. "The Role of Identification in the Post-2015 Development Agenda." World Bank, Washington, DC. http://pubdocs.worldbank.org/en/149911436913670164 /World-Bank-Working-Paper-Center-for-Global-Development-Dahan-Gelb -July2015.pdf

———. 2015d. "WDR16: Spotlight on Digital Identity." World Bank, Washington, DC. http://pubdocs.worldbank.org/en/959381434483205387/WDR16-Spotlight-on -Digital-ID-May-2015-Mariana-Dahan.pdf.

World Health Organization (WHO). 2008. "Health Information Systems: Toolkit on Monitoring Health Systems Strengthening." http://www.who.int/healthinfo/statistics /toolkit_hss/EN_PDF_Toolkit_HSS_InformationSystems.pdf.

Yahya, Yazrina, and Yen Chong. n.d. "Online School Information System Using Web Services Technology to Enhance Smart Teaching and Learning Process." http://www .fp.utm.my/epusatsumber/listseminar/20.konventiontp2007-20/pdf/volume1/10 -yazrina.pdf.

www.ingramcontent.com/pod-product-compliance
Lightning Source LLC
Chambersburg PA
CBHW080418060326
40689CB00019B/4293

9 781464 810565